Uncommon Athletes

By Tim Brown

Endorsements

I have been serving with Tim for nearly 20 years in the Fellowship of Christian Athletes, and the passion he describes of an uncommon athlete, he also portrays as a missionary to our youth and to the sports community. Due to the influence of sports in our society and in the lives of youth, Tim endeavors to equip athletes to leverage their passion to find their God-given purpose, a purpose only found in a relationship with Jesus Christ.

Richard D. Isaiah, FCA Great Lakes
Vice President Field Ministry

With his latest work *Uncommon Athletes*, Tim Brown guides student-athletes down the road to success by helping them find their PASSION and giving them insight through the eyes of many of their sports heroes. A must read for our young athletes!

M. Scott Reeves
Ohio High School Athletic Assoc., Board of Directors

The book, *Uncommon Athletes* is an engaging read. Tim Brown speaks to his audience in-the-now, with powerful, thought provoking logic supported by timely scripture, leaving you with a 'can do' attitude for your own success. The more you read, the more blessed you become and ultimately, you'll find your own personal blueprint.

Greg Turner, Senior Sports Manager for Basketball
Amateur Athletic Union

Tim Brown has a vast amount of experience working with athletes at every level, and from varied backgrounds. His experience becomes ours in *Uncommon Athletes*. This book is a chance for us to learn from one of the best in the business.
Jim Schmidtke, Ohio State University CRU, Athletes in Action

I thought Mr. Brown hit a home run with his last book BOYS WON'T BE BOYS...but *Uncommon Athletes* is a bottom of the ninth grand slam; a posterizing dunk; a fourth and one from the goal line game winning touchdown run! This book is for student athletes of all levels. Anyone who reads it and ACTUALLY applies the contents within will have a successful life on and off the field!
ROY W. HALL, President The Driven Foundation

Tim Brown's *Uncommon Athletes* is one of the best books I have read in some time. As a former collegiate and professional athlete, his candor is refreshing. But as a husband and father to two promising young athletes, Brown's lessons of integrity, sacrifice and selflessness provide a road map to success not only in sports but in life. He masterfully combines storytelling, inspiration, and sincerity with a proper dose of honesty and responsibility. I highly recommend this book to parents with children in any type of organized sport.
Jason Singleton, OSU Athletic Department

FOREWORD
BY CLARK KELLOGG

As the father of 3 Division 1 college athletes, an accomplished hooper in high school, college, and the NBA, and a basketball TV analyst for 30 years, athletics in general and basketball specifically have impacted my life in a permanently positive way for over 40 years. So the enduring life principles that can be gleaned through athletics resonate with me deeply.

Tim Brown has been a friend of mine for more than 25 years and has devoted his life to empowering and inspiring young athletes to lives of purpose and passion, to see athletics in the broader context of being a training ground for life–a means to end, not an end to itself.

Uncommon Athlete is a powerful and practical guide for achieving excellence in how one competes as an athlete AND lives a life of balance, influence and wholeness. Enduring, proven and time-less principles like preparation, attitude, sacrifice, selflessness, integrity, overcoming and nerve are presented in a way to inspire personal application for athletic participation and success and for living one's life well.

Whether you're an athlete, parent of an athlete, coach, teacher or none of the above, the principles and stories in *Uncommon Athlete* can guide and inspire you to reach for the highest levels of successful living and competing–being uncommon.

CONTENTS

INTRODUCTION

It was history. It was drama. It was magic. June 19, 2016. The night the Cleveland Cavaliers won the NBA Championship. They had already done the unthinkable. The first team in NBA history to come back from a 3-1 deficit in the finals, they were tied 3-3 in the series. And with only minutes to go in Game 7, the score was also tied.

And then it happened.

A cross-court power block from LeBron James was the final punch. After a 52 year drought, with a score of 93-89, Cleveland had actually won it all. With tears streaming down his face, LeBron James fell to the floor. He hugged his teammates. He celebrated. And he spoke about what he'd done that night.

I set a goal. Two years...when I came back...to bring a championship to this city. I gave everything I had. I poured my heart and my blood, my sweat and my tears into this game.[1]

The Cavs motto for their run to the Championship was simple: All In. LeBron James led the charge. He was committed to the game, to his team, to his city. He refused to give up. He laid everything on the line in every game, and his entire life can be summed up in a single word: PASSION.

Everyone wants to succeed. You do. I do. There isn't a person in the world who lives each day hoping to fail. But how do we know when we've found success? Is it about your GPA or net worth? Is success limited to those who follow your Instagram account? Thankfully, no, but success is a hard road to climb. And in order to be truly successful, you will have to choose.

Success is like climbing a mountain. To get to the top and look out from the peak is the goal, but on this mountain there are two different paths. Both promise to get us to the top, and both call their destination "success." However, they are not equal roads.

The first defines success by your accomplishments. This is the common road. It's a cookie-cutter path with lots of competition. You're supposed to succeed, to win first place, but everyone else is working for the same goal. And there is only one peak. There is only so much to go around. For me to win, you have to lose. On the common road, everyone is cutthroat, making sure no one gets past them. If you choose this option, you'll never be enough. Not fast enough, winning enough, or rich enough. You will always need more.

But there is another option. It's the uncommon road.

At first glance, it doesn't look like much—a small, barely-trampled path. You can't see all the way to the top. But it's the only sure way to get there. On this road, success looks much different. Instead of everything being a competition, the uncommon road makes everything constructive. It often takes longer. It may require greater sacrifice. It is harder in many ways than the common road, but its payoffs are beyond imagination. Its rewards are immeasurable. The uncommon road is all about true success in every area of life. Especially in the world of sports.

In sports, the common road is everywhere. Common athletes focus on the game. It's all about the stats, the scores, the win column, the championship. On this road, athletes judge their value entirely on performance. Yes, common athletes work hard and play to win. They spend hours honing their skills. They want, with all their heart, to win the big one, break the record, hold the trophy. Some athletes even achieve these goals.

In sports and in life though, the common road will never lead to uncommon success.

Uncommon athletes know that life is more than their sport, more than the championship, more than the final score. Playing uncommonly means that your performance doesn't determine your value. Instead, who you are determines how you play. Uncommon athletes play with excitement, integrity and a vision that goes beyond any single game. Even the championship.

Uncommon athletes always play to win, and they work hard, but instead of being consumed by a sport, these athletes understand that what starts with the team, on the field, in the zone, has to filter out into every area of life. Who he is on the field has to match who he is off the field, too. She recognizes that success on the field will never be enough if she has failed in every other area of life.[2]

So how can an athlete pursue uncommon success? What makes the difference between a life consumed by sports and an athlete constructing a wholehearted life?

The difference is PASSION. Just like LeBron James's passion propelled him to win a championship for his city, passion is the spirit that is filled with drive, zeal, energy, excitement. Passion is the spirit that motivates, compels and moves to action. Passion is the spirit that stirs up and gives fuel to the dream, vision, or goal.

If you want to be uncommon, PASSION must be part of the equation. As the athletes in this book will clearly demonstrate,

PASSION is a powerful foundation for success. It combines wholehearted living and athletic skill into a single unstoppable force. PASSION inspires great plays, great teams, great accomplishments, and great lives.

If you want to be uncommon, you have to choose this path. You have to push toward this goal. You have to discover and apply the seven hallmarks of PASSION:

> Preparation
> Adjustment
> Sacrifice
> Selflessness
> Integrity
> Overcoming
> Nerve

That is the game plan for this book. In each chapter, we will break down one quality. We will look at what it is, what it looks like on the field or court and how it plays into all of life, so that any athlete, in any sport, can pursue the uncommon path.

Every athlete has to be driven. She will have to be dedicated. He will have to be devoted. But to be uncommon, on the field and in life, an athlete must ignite PASSION. It will move him to play and live with everything he has. It will define her as a leader, on and off the field. That PASSION will ignite the team and the community to play and be better, too.

And that is uncommon.

Chapter 1

UNCOMMON PREPARATION

*The fortuity of life comes more often as preparation
becomes a practice.*

First Steps

The first element of PASSION is preparation. If you do not come
to the game prepared, you cannot succeed. It is that simple. And
that hard.

Jerry Rice is one of the greatest wide receivers ever to play
professional football. He played in the NFL for over twenty years,
was a Super Bowl MVP, and racked up over 200 touchdowns,
1,500 receptions, and 22,000 receiving yards in his career.

Jerry Rice is a highly talented football player, but he did not
become the most effective wide receiver in NFL history only
because of his talent. Instead, his success was a direct result of the
thousands of hours he spent preparing for every game, every
season. "I don't think I'm such a natural; I think what I'm doing
is very hard work. I work hard to keep in shape, I work hard on
the practice field, I work hard in a game. It isn't easy."[1]

Preparation isn't easy, but it's important. And it's very, very
uncommon.

The Mindset of Preparation

Preparation always begins with a plan. This is the uncommon
mindset. Any athlete can swagger into the weight room and start
lifting, but without a goal there's no real point. To be truly
prepared, you need a plan.

Your plan is the roadmap to get you from where you are today, to where you want to be someday. It is a powerful guide that will keep you focused when you're stuck and keep you on track to reach your goals. It tells your starting point, your end goal and which steps you need to take to bridge the gap. And with it, you will find a clear path toward your highest goals.[2]

Start where you are right now. In order to plan effectively, you have to assess your skill level and capabilities today. Are you 5-foot-4 and 125 pounds? Great. Do you currently run a 6-minute mile? Fantastic. This part of the plan is not about judging; it's about truth. Don't beat yourself up over your current numbers or stats. Just take an honest look at yourself and your skills.

Next, decide where you want to end up. Do you need to gain fifteen pounds to play the position you want? Do you need to shave seconds (or minutes) off your sprint time? Do you want to have the stats to earn a Division I scholarship? Write down, as clearly as you can, exactly what you want to achieve. That is your goal.

Last, how do you get from today to the end goal? Ask your coaches or trainers to help you. Bring your parents into the discussion.[3] Write down specific steps for each part of your goal. Make the plan clear, concise, and realistic. Know what you intend to achieve and write out a clear pathway to that goal.

The Power of Consistency

Once you have a plan, preparation becomes entirely about your will. You have to have the discipline to follow through on your plan. The word is consistency.

Consistency is a faithfulness in how you do something or in what you think. You stick to it. No matter how tempting it is to do something different or choose an easier way, a consistent person stays on course.

Emmitt Smith spent fifteen seasons proving he is one of the greatest football players ever to compete. He is the all-time rushing leader in the NFL. He had eleven straight 1,000-yard rushing seasons and helped propel the Dallas Cowboys into three Super Bowls in four years.[4]

In his Hall of Fame induction speech, Smith described the reasons for his success. "Another critical principle is consistency. Consistency shows value. Consistency is necessary for trust, durability and longevity. You have to show up every week no matter how difficult the game or life might be. Over time consistency will allow you to achieve your goals."[5]

Let's break that down.

First, consistency "shows value." Basically, this means that how you spend your time or money reveals what you value. We will always spend time on what's truly important. If you play games on your phone instead of shooting free throws after dinner, if you get up early to train before school, if you do your homework before practice, it'll be easy to see what really matters. The choices you make, over and over, show what you value.

Second, consistency "is necessary for trust, durability and longevity." In other words, you prove yourself by being consistent. When you're consistent, your teammates trust you. When you train consistently, you develop physical durability and longevity in your sport. Consistency is vital.

Last, it is consistency that will allow you to achieve your goals. The only way to accomplish whatever goal you set for yourself is the slow, methodical path of consistency. To be ready on game night, you can't practice free throws once a week; you have to shoot from the line every day. It's also about more than repetition—just doing something over and over. Uncommon consistency means doing that skill *the right way* over and over. Correcting your grip, your stance, your lunge, your stride—and doing it repeatedly in the correct way—is how consistency will benefit you the most.

This level of consistency is what make the uncommon athlete truly powerful. He is always ready. He can jump into the game at a moment's notice. She can pick up the ball, come off the bench, or fill in for an injury. Because of her consistency, she is confident in her ability to perform every time.

Preparation begins with a plan and is built on consistency, but how do you put uncommon preparation into practice? There are two basic steps that will help you succeed.

Step One: Show Up
An uncommon athlete comes to practice. Every practice. He comes to every meeting and conditioning session. Every chance she gets to prepare, she is there, ready to go, and she stays until the end. Uncommon athletes know the unwritten practice standard: to be early is to be on time, to be on time is to be late, and to be late is to be left behind.

Long before he won his 23 gold medals, Michael Phelps showed up. During his teens, Michael Phelps trained *every day* for 6 years; that's more than 2,100 days straight![6] Whether he wanted to or not, he showed up to swim. Whether it was a good practice or not, he swam. When he was sick and when he was tired and when he was having a really great day, Michael Phelps got in the pool. He showed up.

The key word is *choice*. You cannot just want to be good. You cannot just hope to become uncommon. You have to choose, and the choice is really about time.

Think about it. Every person on the planet gets 24 hours every day. That's 1,440 minutes. Every day. But what you do with that time is what makes the difference. Most people will waste their time, lost in games or screens or Instagram selfies. But you can learn to use time well. You can use it wisely.

We learn to use our time wisely by considering how fast it goes and how quickly it runs out. We begin to recognize, along with Dr. Benjamin Mays, the power of a single minute. He wrote:

> I have only just a minute,
> Only sixty seconds in it.
> Forced upon me, can't refuse it.
> Didn't seek it, didn't choose it.
> But it's up to me
> to use it.
> I must suffer if I lose it.
> Give account if I abuse it.
> Just a tiny little minute,
> But eternity is in it.[7]

Until we learn to count our time as more valuable than money, we will waste it. Until we learn to number our days well—understanding that no one knows when their last moment will come—we will live foolishly. But when we recognize that we have only a limited amount of time, we will begin to live well. Because we will *choose* to live it well.[8]

Wise or foolish, the choice is yours alone. It's easy to rely on a parent or coach to tell you what to do and when to do it. But that is not uncommon. In order to be uncommon, in order to be prepared, you have choose for yourself. You have to give your time to whatever goal you want to achieve, and you are going to have to give it even when you really wish you were doing something else.

Phelps made that wise choice 2,100 times in a row, and he was more than prepared when it was time to compete. Every athlete with PASSION does the same. Allyson Felix, who has won six Olympic gold medals, said, "To me, the competing is the easy part. It's putting in the work, those long hours on the track, all year long. That's where those medals are won."[9]

Uncommon preparation means you show up. It means setting aside time for conditioning and drills. It's making a schedule and being disciplined enough to follow it. Uncommon preparation means assigning specific moments of your day to prepare: going over tape, working on your weak areas, building in muscle memory. It may mean getting up early or staying after school or going back out after dinner, but preparation means showing up, and showing up always requires time. When you are pursuing uncommon preparation, you have to choose to give that time, ahead of time.

Step Two: Push Yourself.
Showing up is important, but simply being there is not enough. Some athletes show up like their presence is a gift to the coach or the team. It's not. Bad attitudes, ego trips and negativity

undermine uncommon preparation every time. Instead, you have to give it all. Legendary coach Bobby Knight once said, "The key is not the will to win...everybody has that. It is the will to prepare to win that is important."[10]

Jerry Rice prepared on "the Hill" in San Francisco. Every day, Rice ran 2.5 miles uphill without stopping, even during the off-season. He said, "A lot of professional players would wait until training camp to work themselves into shape. I would take two weeks off during the off-season, then go right back into my regimen."[11] Rice pushed himself, and when the time came to perform, he was ready. Every time.

Uncommon athletes prepare to win. They work hard at every drill. No matter how many laps or up-downs the coaches demand, they do them. And like Jerry Rice, they keep pushing themselves even when others take an easier road.

To be uncommon, you have to push yourself. You have to do better, be better, win better. You must work hard to learn the skills and mental strength you'll need in competition because once the competition starts, it's better to have it and not need it than need it and not be prepared for it. Pushing yourself in practice means you will have the power and instinct to be great when it matters most.

Preparation in Practice
However … let's be honest. That moment when preparation turns into action can be intimidating.

At some point, every athlete must turn hard work into actual game experience. Tension builds as the entire team waits in position for the ref's whistle. The runners stand poised in the starting blocks. The archer notches an arrow and takes aim. And the question stands: will their preparation really be enough?

Faced with their big moment, many athletes choke. Even after they've spent a thousand hours honing their skills, teams and athletes simply fall apart. In Cleveland, for example, there is The Catch, The Shot, The Fumble, The Drive—moments that are seared into people's memory of when their team, once again, crumbled when the pressure was on. But no matter your sport, no matter your level of play, no matter your history, that moment when you must put your preparation into action *can* be conquered.

1. **Focus on the moment.** The purpose of preparation is to make each skill a habit, so you don't have to think about it during the game. When you start to analyze what you're doing, you throw off that habit. Find ways to stay focused, to do the routine or run the race exactly as you practiced, without letting your brain sabotage the effort.

2. **Don't Compare.** You can only do what you can do. Don't worry about the other team's record or the other runner's time. You cannot control anything about the opponent. Focus instead on yourself, on your warm-up routine and your team's readiness to play. That is what you can control, so don't compare.

3. **Have fun.** Playing a sport is supposed to be fun. You should do it because you love it. If the pressure starts to grow, find ways to go back to the fun side of things. Play a pick-up game. Play a completely different sport. Dance around to fun music to lighten things up. Restoring the fun of the game will help you live the moments of the game more fully.[12]

Steve Nash, former NBA point guard, once said, "You have to rely on your preparation. You got to really be passionate and try to prepare more than anyone else, putting yourself in a position to succeed, so when the moment comes you got to enjoy, relax, breathe and rely on your preparation so you can perform and not be anxious or filled with doubt."[13] Uncommon preparation will help you play to the best of your ability and enjoy the experience, too.

The Power of Preparation
Uncommon preparation is possible. It takes a combination of planning, discipline and follow-through, but it is possible. And when you prepare at this level, you'll achieve powerful results.

Powerful Teams
Uncommon preparation is the foundation of unstoppable teams. They work together to reach their goals, and the result is a team that can accomplish anything. Even more, the group supports and strengthens each member. When a day comes, as it always does, where one of the team wants to quit early, give up, or drop out, the other members encourage him to stay focused and keep going. Uncommon preparation ensures that the team becomes as strong as it can possibly be.

Powerful Possibilities
Uncommon preparation also opens up amazing possibilities. For any athlete, success and glory are possible, but they are more likely to come when you work hard to achieve them. Golfing legend Gary Player commented, "The harder you work, the luckier you get."[14] Uncommon athletes practice hard at every level because they understand that today's preparation leads to tomorrow's victories. They develop the habits of planning and consistency, showing up and pushing hard, from peewee league

to varsity, because they know talent is never enough to ensure final victory. Uncommon athletes know they must always come prepared.

Powerful Influence.
Finally, Uncommon athletes prepare to become leaders. Uncommon preparation will always produce a superior athlete who is effective during competition and quickly becomes a leader on the team. The coach trusts him, knowing he has practiced faithfully and is ready to compete. Her teammates depend on her because they know she'll show up and play well.

In any sport, the uncommon athlete is irreplaceable, a secret weapon ready to be used as soon as the opportunity presents itself. That is the power of preparation.

TALK About It
1. Do you have a plan to accomplish your athletic goals? Why can't an athlete just "wing it" and still pursue uncommon preparation?

2. Why is it hard for most athletes to live out uncommon preparation? Which part is hardest for you personally: making a plan, being consistent, showing up, or pushing yourself?

3. Re-read the poem in the "Showing Up" section. What lines struck you most in this poem? What does "eternity is in it" mean? Consider your own minutes. Do you use your time well?

4. Uncommon preparation makes you powerful. Which result (powerful teams, powerful possibilities, powerful influence) do you think brings the greatest rewards? Why?

5. How can you apply the principles discussed in this chapter to areas of your life outside of sports? What does uncommon preparation look like at home, at school, at work, or in other areas of life?

Chapter 2

UNCOMMON ATTITUDE (ADJUSTMENT)

*If you're adaptable and nimble, that's great, because
that's exactly what life requires you to be.*

A Change of Plans

In 2014, Lauren Hill was a high school senior. She was looking
forward to graduation, and she was planning to play basketball
for Mount St. Joseph University in the fall. But those plans
changed unexpectedly when a visit to her doctor revealed she
had a brain tumor. An inoperable brain tumor.

Further tests revealed that she had a rare form of cancer, and she
was given less than two years to live. Instead of quitting, Lauren
adjusted. She continued to play basketball, fighting through the
negative effects of her tumor. She started a nonprofit organization
to raise money and awareness for the cancer she was fighting.
And that fall, she started school at Mount St. Joseph anyway,
playing in their season opener (which the NCAA allowed them
to play early because of her illness).[1]

Lauren refused to let a terminal diagnosis bench her. Though the
cancer progressed quickly, and she passed away on April 10,
2015, her life was marked by an unbeatable attitude. She did not
shrink from difficulty. Instead, she accepted the change, adjusted
her plan, and kept on living (and playing) an uncommon life.

Oaks and Palms

The first hallmark of an uncommon athlete is preparation, and Lauren Hill was prepared. She knew what she wanted, and she had a clear plan to get there. But the truth is, life does not always go according to plan. It didn't for Lauren, and it won't for you either.

In the middle of a game, plans will suddenly shift. The coach will change a play. The ref's call will go against your team, ending a drive or erasing a score. The unexpected will happen, and you will face injuries, miscommunication, equipment trouble, or coaching errors. Without warning, something in the plan will change, and you will have to figure out how to respond.

Other difficulties will come from outside your sport. That was Lauren Hill's story, and it might be yours, too. You may face a difficult home life or struggle in your classes. Your storms might come from relationships or the consequences of a bad decision. But whatever roadblocks come your way, you can find true success despite your circumstances, even very difficult ones.

The key is your attitude. The uncommon athlete has an attitude that adjusts.

Attitude is the way you see your circumstances. It is what determines how you respond to your circumstances, and it is the only part of your circumstances that you can actually control.

Having an attitude of adjustment means you willingly choose to alter or adapt your current plan so you can pursue true success despite your circumstances. And an uncommon athlete must develop this uncommon attitude. Without it, you will never survive the storms that come.

Think about an oak tree. Its wood is stiff; its trunk solid. Now imagine a hurricane blasting the tree. Oaks survive by putting down deep roots and holding on tightly underground, but a big storm puts that tree at great risk. Faced with gale-force winds, the tree will eventually break, torn to pieces by the tension between its roots buried deep in the ground and the power of the wind.

The same is true for athletes who can't adjust. When hard times come their way, they break. They feel the game shift, the momentum change, the opponent rally, and they go stiff, trying to fight back. They plant their roots and hold on, but eventually they crumble beneath the pressure.

Uncommon athletes, on the other hand, do not crumble. They are like a palm tree. A palm tree can bend along with a hurricane's winds, and because it bends it can withstand the storm. The wind pushes against palm trees with the same force that destroyed the oak. But because the palm tree allows the wind to move it, just a little bit it survives. It might lose a few leaves, but it adjusts to its new reality.

That's the attitude Lauren Hill displayed. She did not choose to have a rare and inoperable brain tumor, but when one appeared, she adjusted. She didn't give up. She fought her cancer as well as she could. She kept living, even as her tumor grew, but she adjusted her plan to fit her new reality. She became a coach when she could no longer play. She used her story to raise money and awareness for research. It wasn't her Plan A, but she found a new path through her storm, and she followed it. She adjusted, and her uncommon attitude allowed her to respond positively, proactively and powerfully to very bad circumstances.

Plan B

An attitude that adjusts is really about being flexible. It means staying open to the possibility that things will change. Yes, you must have a plan; that's part of being prepared. But you cannot hold too tightly to your roadmap. You must keep a flexible attitude toward that plan so that, when something in your life changes, you can shift gears and move to Plan B.[2]

Of course, few athletes, even uncommon ones, have a Plan B ready to go when circumstances change. Most difficulties blindside us, and it can be hard to shift. Our instinct will be to hold tightly to our original plan. Without adjustment, we become rigid (like an oak tree), and we will break before we can find a new way. That's why flexibility is so important. It helps us think outside the box. It enables us to respond creatively to our problem. It helps us switch gears before we break so we can continue to move forward.

Flexibility also allows uncommon athletes to move through difficulties at their own pace. We always want hard stuff to disappear *right.this.second*, but it takes time to come up with a new plan that will actually work. And that is okay. Give yourself that time. When circumstances change or difficulties comes, remember that it is wise to step back, take time to evaluate, and then move forward in a new direction.[3]

In 2014, Braxton Miller was the quarterback of the Ohio State Buckeyes. He was a powerhouse of college football and an early Heisman favorite, but just days before the season opener, Miller injured the shoulder of his throwing arm and missed the entire season.

When he returned, two other quarterbacks were vying for the

starting position. With his arm still not at full strength, Miller crafted Plan B. He secretly made plans to change positions from quarterback to wide receiver.[4] He knew it was risky. Very few college athletes have switched positions and made it in the NFL. But he was willing to try. He learned new skills and worked hard, with no promises that he would make it to the pros, but he did it. In May 2016, he was drafted by the Houston Texans as a wide receiver.[5]

Braxton Miller had an attitude of adjustment. With one throw, his entire life changed. He had been training to be a quarterback for years, and suddenly, he had months to learn how to be a capable wide receiver. He was flexible. He put down his original plan and started looking at alternatives. He formed a new plan, then he pursued his Plan B with the same tenacity he had always shown.

Learning to Adjust
Like Braxton Miller, an uncommon athlete is able to adjust, but adjusting isn't easy. To successfully flex when tough times come, you need two important things: perspective and persistence.

Perspective
Having perspective means seeing today's plan without losing sight of the long-term goals. Even though he had injured his arm, Braxton Miller still wanted to play in the NFL. So he changed his plans to make that happen. The goal stayed the same, but the path to the goal shifted. An uncommon athlete will always keep his focus on his final goal—the championship, the win, the record—but he doesn't lose perspective. He knows there are many paths he can take to get there, and when circumstances change, he finds a new path to that goal.

However, the ultimate goal of an uncommon athlete is not about the win-loss record. She knows that life is much bigger than a single game or trophy. Uncommon athletes know the plan for this game and this season, but they always keep the big picture in view, too. Yes, they want to win the game, but they also want to be a winner at life. They want to make the big plays, but not at the risk of injury to themselves or others. They believe in themselves, but they know cockiness is not the same thing as confidence. They have true perspective.

Persistence

Making adjustments, whether during a game or in life, is hard. If you expect your opponents to play a fast game, but they run a slow offense to throw you off, it can be hard to adjust your game plan. When the doctor tells you the bad diagnosis, your parents decide to divorce, or the teacher announces a pop quiz, it will knock you, at least momentarily, to the mat.

Persistence will help you keep going, even if it doesn't look pretty. Adjusting takes time and effort. You will make many mistakes. But you cannot give up. Braxton Miller was persistent in the face of his circumstances. For months, he practiced secretly, late at night, learning new routes, new stances, a new way of seeing the field before he announced the change. It was frustrating. He missed being the quarterback. There was no guarantee it would work. At times, it would have been easier for him to give up. But his persistence made it possible for him to adjust. That's what an uncommon athlete does.

Getting Practical

Even with perspective and persistence, your natural response to bad things happening is not going to be uncommon adjustment. Unless we choose differently, we will usually respond by whining, getting angry, throwing punches, throwing a fit, or generally feeling sorry for ourselves. It would be great if uncommon adjustment just happened, but that is not how it works.

You have to *learn* to adjust. And that happens exactly like learning the basic skills of your sport. It is slow. It starts with mastering the basics and then moving up to more advanced skills. In the same way, you have to practice adjusting. You have to build up your adjustment muscles. It takes time and effort, but there are three habits you can practice every day that will help you develop this uncommon attitude.

1. Be Proactive, Not Reactive.

Our emotions are important. They help us respond to what we experience. A funeral makes us feel sad. Our team wins, and we're happy. Disrespect makes us angry. We need emotions. Without them, we could not be uncommon. But we cannot let our emotions run the show, and they cannot dictate our choices.[6]

Our emotions change constantly. They are color commentators on our lives, giving a play-by-play of what we experience. They tell us about this one moment, how we feel *right now*. And that is their weakness. Emotions tell us how to feel, not what to do. So if we decide what to do based on how we feel *right.this.second*, we are reactive, not proactive.

To be reactive means that we wait for something to happen and then respond to it. Being proactive means we act, choosing a path forward for ourselves, even when we don't "feel" like doing it. We can feel sad but choose to be kind to someone else. We can be angry but choose not to share our grumpy mood. We can feel cheated when the ref makes a bad call, but still be respectful and play well. That's what it means to be proactive.

Being proactive means we rise above what it happening to us; it is *how* we adjust. We decide in our minds to deal with hard circumstances without responding in a knee-jerk way. We acknowledge honestly what is happening and how we feel about it, but then we decide to do what we need to do. That decision keeps us from being trapped by our emotions. It enables us to bend and flex, moving us past how the situation feels to a Plan B that will get us back on track toward our goal.

2. Don't Compare.

Comparison robs us of our ability to adjust. The more you let what you do depend on other people, the more trapped and dependent you become on them. When someone else dictates your choices, you become a puppet. If someone else tells you what to wear, how to spend Friday night, or which friends you are supposed to talk to (or avoid), then you are trapped in someone else's rules. And that is not uncommon.

We have to practice keeping our focus on our own lives and our own choices. When you choose not to compare your life to other people's lives, you are free to adjust whenever you need to. Do not let others define your choices. Don't compare. Just be yourself. Focus on doing your own thing and doing it to the best of your ability, so that when you face difficulties you are free to adjust … on your own terms.

3. Develop Resilience

Just like a gymnast slowly stretches her muscles over time until she can perform the most advanced maneuvers, you can gradually stretch your own internal muscles to develop an attitude of adjustment. This internal flexibility is called *resilience*.

Resilience is the ability to bounce back, recover, or let something roll off your back. Resilience means you have the will to stand up again after being knocked down. It's like dropping a bucket into a deep well and pulling up exactly the resources you need to handle any situation you face.

Resilience factors are life skills; they are tools you keep ready until you need them. Some resilience factors will be part of your personality naturally, some of them you will have to develop intentionally, but the more of these life skills you have, the better able you will be to adjust when life changes. Here are some good examples:

- Time management skills
- Good communication skills
- The ability to set and reach goals
- The ability to problem solve
- Self-confidence
- The ability to predict
- A sense of humor
- Faith or religious connections
- Strong (and healthy) connections to family and friends[7]

Resilience is a powerful tool for an uncommon life. Instead of working to avoid hard things, resilience helps you go through them. And "going through" is important. Going through tough times teaches us to persevere. It helps us see that we *can* persevere, we don't have to take the easy way out, we are strong enough to forge ahead and win. Perseverance builds our character. When we go through the hard stuff, we become people of value and substance. And as we develop character, we gain hope. We'll know that, whatever the future holds, we will find the way through.[8] This is the power of resilience.

Be proactive, don't compare and develop resilience. These are the habits that will help every uncommon athlete learn to adjust. When hard times come, he doesn't whine or wallow in self-pity. Instead, she chooses to face her situation and find a way around the problem. He comes up with a Plan B and follows it wholeheartedly.

Adjustment is not the norm. It won't be easy at first. But with practice and flexibility, you can develop this uncommon attitude and keep yourself moving toward your goal.

TALK About It

1. Are you more like an oak tree or a palm tree? Are you good at making adjustments, or do you prefer to have a plan and stick to it?

2. Why is it so important to develop an attitude that can adjust in sports? How is it also important in other areas: at school, for a job, at home or in relationships?

3. Is it hard to be persistent? How can you motivate yourself to keep going in moments when you feel like giving up?

4. Look again at the list of resilience factors. Which ones do you naturally do well? Which can you work on so that you have a full toolbox to draw from when difficulties come?

5. "We cannot control our circumstances, but we can control our attitude." Do you agree or disagree? How can you apply this principle when changes come into your life?

Chapter 3

UNCOMMON SACRIFICE

*Surrendering yourself for a greater good isn't giving up who you are;
it's the master key to discovering who you can be.*

Everything Comes Second

Uncommon Athletes are defined by PASSION. They prepare. They develop an attitude that adjusts. Even more importantly, they sacrifice.

In 2015, Carli Lloyd scored three goals against Japan in the first sixteen minutes of the World Cup finals, making her the first woman ever to score a hat trick in the finals. The team dominated Japan because of her playmaking, and she was named FIFA World Player of the Year.[1]

Lloyd's success was not an accident. She began training for that finals win in 2003 after she was cut from the USWNT's Under-21 team. She made a seventeen-year plan to become a world-class athlete, and her plan is built on sacrifice. She trains twice a day, nearly every day. She pushes herself mentally and physically to strengthen her game. She trains like an underdog and constantly raises the bar. And after her World Cup win, she declared, "I've dedicated my whole life to this. Everything comes second."[2]

Everything comes second. That is the attitude of uncommon sacrifice. Lloyd has a plan with clear goal that she is pursuing wholeheartedly. The hours of practice, the physical challenges, the mental effort cost her time and energy and even tears, but they are all worth it because they help her achieve great things.

No Exceptions

Sacrifice is the surrender of one thing for something else. Something better. It means knowing what you want more than anything, and then giving up whatever will keep you from that goal. In sports, the goal is often a championship, a winning season or a trophy. Whatever the goal, sacrifice will be part of the journey to get there.

Even the superstar athletes, the ones who make success look easy, have to give their time, their money, their everything to their success. Michael Jordan, Tiger Woods and Peyton Manning reached the highest levels of success in their sports, but they had to sacrifice as much, if not more, than everyone else. Muhammad Ali once said, "I hated every minute of training, but I said, 'Don't quit. Suffer now and live the rest of your life as a champion.'"[3] Ali understood sacrifice. He didn't feel like training, but he did it anyway. He worked harder and practiced longer, and in the end, his sacrifice got him exactly where he wanted to go.

Unfortunately, many athletes at every level want to reach their goals without sacrifice. They don't want to train, to run, to push themselves. They are content with their natural abilities. They ease up. They do the bare minimum and hope it is enough, but it won't be. As Kareem Abdul-Jabbar said, "I think that the good and the great are only separated by the willingness to sacrifice."[4]

Uncommon athletes want to be great, and they understand that the only place success comes before work is in the dictionary. It is through hard work and sacrifice that an athlete is crafted. Like a blacksmith shapes metal with heat and pressure into anything he wants to create, uncommon sacrifice forms the athlete into a powerful and effective competitor. It is only through sacrifice that a player can develop fully, focus completely, and achieve great things. It is part of the equation. No exceptions.

The Cost of Sacrifice

As much as we need to sacrifice, sacrifice is hard. It always comes at a price. You have to give something up to get something you want more.

It's a question of values. We all value certain things: family, sportsmanship, a winning season, faith. We know what we want. We know what our priorities are, but we can't do it all. No one can. Hard as we try, we cannot schedule our time to fit in all the important things in our lives. To win the championship, you must give up other things. To be great on the field, you may not also be able to have a job. To support the team, you may have to give up opportunities to get individual recognition. We cannot have it all. So we must choose. That choice is where the sacrifice actually happens.

Shawn Johnson, who won Olympic gold in gymnastics in 2008, described it this way, "I don't call them sacrifices. I call them exchanges. I've had to exchange a lot of family time, friend time, school time, and social time for gym time. I was never able to pull an all-nighter with my friends because I had to exchange those moments to be up early the next day for practice."[5] Sacrifice means trading one valuable thing for another. You must make the exchange.

Chris Spielman learned this the hard way. He was a formidable lineman at every level of football. He gave his time and energy to play well, and he excelled in high school, college, and the NFL. When his wife, Stefanie, was diagnosed with breast cancer, though, he found a higher priority. As much as he loved football, he missed the 1998 season to help his wife fight her disease.

That is sacrifice. That's what it looks like to give something up, something we want very much, in order to pursue something better. And the truth is, no one can become great without giving up lesser things first.

Chris Spielman understood that idea on the football field, but after he retired, he realized that sacrifice applies in life, as well. As Stefanie's cancer progressed, he prioritized family over football. He learned to ask for help instead of pushing through on his own. And even though Chris lost Stefanie to cancer in 2009, Spielman gained much from his sacrifice on her behalf. He gained faith, patience and a lifelong mission to fight against cancer with the same passion he displayed on the football field. To him, the sacrifice was worth it.[6]

Sacrifice isn't easy. It means making hard trades, giving up your time or energy or something you want in order to gain something better. It costs us greatly to sacrifice, but when we do, we learn to give up what is lesser for what is truly important, and we will be able to rise to greater heights and face greater challenges than ever before.

Focus on the Harvest

In many ways the farmer and the athlete are surprisingly similar. They both put in long hours of hard and lonely work. They have to wait for their rewards. They both must also understand the power of uncommon sacrifice.

In farming, the principle of sacrifice is best seen in growing crops. It's the idea of sowing and reaping. Instead of demanding instant results, like microwave popcorn, the farmer sacrifices time and energy today for a harvest that won't come for weeks or months.

The farmer knows that sacrifice right now will ensure a better crop in the future. He plants, he waters, he weeds, he waits, and finally, at the very end, he harvests. He does this, year after year, because he understands the truth about reaping a harvest.

You reap *only* what you sow.
You always reap *later* than you sow.
You always reap *more* than you sow.

An athlete must learn the same truths. You reap *only* what you sow. No athlete will gain a reward he hasn't worked for. Yes, there are naturally gifted players, but unless they perfect their skills, they will never achieve all that they are capable of achieving. You cannot harvest what you haven't put in.[7]

You always reap *later* than you sow. No athlete will earn the medal before they've run the race. Even though one team is "sure" to win, the game must be played before the win can be recorded. The same is true for practicing. You cannot cut seconds off your record before you train your body. You must do the work first, and later you will receive the reward.[8]

Lastly, you always reap *more* than you sow. On a farm, each single seed produces a plant with large amounts of fruit. One seed equals bushels of harvest. The benefits of sacrifice may not come immediately, but they will come. And when they do, they are often much more than a mere trophy or championship. The rewards of uncommon sacrifice will overflow into every area of your life: reputation, school, home, leadership, community influence. You will gain much more from your sacrifices than you can possibly imagine.[9]

Like a farmer preparing his fields, the uncommon athlete understands that what you put into something always determines what you get out of it. Uncommon sacrifice means looking ahead and choosing wisely today to ensure great victory at the end.

Practical Sacrifice

So to be uncommon, we must sacrifice. It isn't easy. We'd rather eat ice cream than go work out one more time. We'd rather focus on our own reputation and leave our teammates to worry about theirs, but sacrifice must happen. To become sacrificial, you have to learn three basic principles.

1. Begin with the End in Mind

Sacrifice is easier if you know exactly what you're sacrificing for, what your plan is. Shawn Johnson had Olympic gold as her goal, so exchanging friend time for gym time was a choice she was willing to make. An uncommon athlete does the same. You have to plan in reverse. Start with your end goal and work backward until you know exactly what you have to do today to reach that goal someday.

That's what the NFL tells each year's rookies. Every summer, new players are required to attend a four-day training session where former players and staff talk about the reality of a professional football career. The common theme is "begin with the end in mind." Players like Eddie George and Aeneas Williams challenge the rookies to consider, even before their first training camp, what they want their life to look like at the end of their career. If they want to wear the Hall of Fame jacket, if they want to be a success after retiring, if they want to stay in the league more than three years, then they will have to make choices, today, to get them where they want to go.[10]

Every uncommon athlete lives this way. See the end you want, and live today to make that end happen. Those choices will require sacrifice, but when you know *why* you're making the exchange, you will be much more willing to try.[11]

2. No Shortcuts

Sacrifice means taking the hard road. It means refusing to short circuit the work required to reach your goals. Uncommon athletes know this and are disciplined enough to follow through. They don't always like it, but they do it anyway. Apolo Ohno, former Olympic speed skater, said, "We all naturally want to become successful ... we also want to take shortcuts. And it's easy to do so, but you can never take away the effort of hard work and discipline and sacrifice."[12]

For uncommon athletes, there are no shortcuts. As tempting as it may be to take performance-enhancing drugs or try to fast-track your training regimen, the uncommon athlete knows it isn't worth it in the end. True success requires sacrifice and discipline. Doing the slow, steady work of training well, practicing hard and overcoming your weaknesses is the only way to true success.

In sports, there is always a cost. Uncommon athletes pay the cost up front, but athletes who cheat still sacrifice. They may avoid some sweat and hard work, but they will pay, just in a different way. Marion Jones was a world-class athlete with Olympic medals and an established reputation, but doping cost her every title, every medal. She spent six months in jail and had to publicly apologize. She took a shortcut and paid a much higher price in the long run.[13]

There are no shortcuts to being uncommon.

3. Delayed Gratification

Delayed gratification is a big phrase with a simple meaning: waiting until later to get something that you want right now.

That's it. It's another way of saying that you "made the exchange," but what sounds simple is one of the hardest things any athlete can learn to do.

Developing the skill of delayed gratification takes time and practice. It's a slow muscle to build. If you already know you have no tolerance for waiting, start with something small. Wait ten minutes before you eat dessert. Count to five before you respond to someone's question. Read five more pages of your English homework before you pick up your phone.

Start small and work your way up. Make little sacrifices until waiting for what you want becomes more natural to you. Then do a little bit more. Do two more reps of each practice drill before you move on. Run one extra lap. Add one harder move to your training regimen.

The power of delayed gratification will change your life. It is the heart of uncommon sacrifice, and it is the foundation of an uncommon life.

Uncommon Sacrifice

No success will ever come without sacrifice. It's true in practice and in the weight room, but it's even more true in life. Sacrificing for your sport is a valuable thing. Giving your all to win the championship is good, but sacrifice is always bigger than your sport.

Sacrifice is especially important in the area of education. For better or worse, most people will succeed or fail based on their education. While there are exceptions, a person who barely passes or drops out of high school will face a difficult future. So many athletes illustrate this view. They succeed on the field, moving swiftly from high school, to college, to the pros. But with no education to stand on, when their career is done, they struggle to succeed.

Vince Carter took this truth seriously. When he left college early to play in the NBA, his mother made him promise he would go back and finish his degree. He did, he finished his classes and received his diploma at graduation in May 2001–before playing in an NBA playoff game that night! Though his team lost the game by one point and others criticized his decision to go to graduation, Carter knew what was important, and he was willing to sacrifice to get it done.[14]

As hard as it is to be diligent in school, an uncommon athlete focuses on scholarship *and* athletics. Like Vince Carter, you must sacrifice in both areas to create a healthy balance. Don't focus on the weight room to the exclusion of your homework. Don't sacrifice your school work for your sports dreams. Make both a priority so you can set yourself up for a lifetime of success, on and off the field.

In every area of life, no matter your goal–beating that video game, getting an A, making a difference in your school or neighborhood–it can only be achieved with uncommon sacrifice. Give up lesser things so you have time and energy to do better things. Don't watch TV so you can do your homework. Save your cash instead of spending it. Stay home on Saturday night so you don't get sucked into unwise or illegal things. Those uncommon sacrifices will build toward great success, in sports and in life.

TALK About It

1. We sacrifice for whatever we think is truly important. Do you agree or not?

2. How does focusing on your end goal help you sacrifice today? Can you ever sacrifice too much for your goal?

3. Sacrifice is about giving up lesser things now for something better in the future. What are some "lesser gains" that might tempt you to avoid sacrifice?

4. How good are you at delayed gratification? What is one small change you can make to start developing the habit more fully in your life?

5. How well do you sacrifice for school or family or other areas of life? Is it easier to sacrifice for sports? Why?

Chapter 4

UNCOMMON SELFLESSNESS

When you become a selfless team, you'll soon be a winning team.

A Missing Piece

An uncommon athlete has PASSION. He is prepared. She adjusts. These athletes sacrifice. With that said, you can be marked by all of those qualities and still be missing an important aspect of PASSION. Perhaps the most important element is uncommon selflessness.

Mia Hamm was a superstar in women's soccer for nearly twenty years. She was unstoppable on the field and a worldwide favorite. Along with her teammates, she built the USWNT into an international success, winning the World Cup in 1991 and 1999 and two Olympic gold medals in 1996 and 2004. On the field, she was known for her skill and control, and she scored over 150 goals in international play.[1]

Mia understood the team came first. As often as she scored, she also passed, assisting her teammates in their scoring drives. She also recognized that her own accomplishments were never the point. "I am a member of a team, and I rely on the team, I defer to it and sacrifice for it, because the team, not the individual, is the ultimate champion."[2]

Asking the Wrong Questions

Unfortunately, Hamm's attitude is not the norm. In most sports today, selfishness is the name of the game. Selfishness is the "concern for one's own welfare or advantage at the expense of or in disregard of others."[3] Simply put, it's making *your* best interests a higher priority than anything else.

We see it everywhere. College teams are built on the reputations of one or two players who run up their stats and then leave the team and their schooling to turn pro early. Professional athletes try to dominate, on the court or with endorsements, without concern for the rest of the team. Players are consumed with their own skills, their own performance, their own success. They focus on their goals, and even in team sports they function as if they are the most important person in the game.

The truth is, every athlete, even uncommon ones, can struggle with selfish attitudes. It's easier to see in others. That's why we criticize college and professional athletes for selfishness, but any athlete at any level can become selfish. I can. So can you. We must learn to recognize selfishness in our lives, not just point out how it shows up in someone else's.[4]

Selfishness happens when your priorities aren't right. What you want becomes more important than your friends and family. Staying out of trouble is more important than protecting your sister, so you blame her for the broken lamp. You behave selfishly. It works the same in sports. When getting what you want (your goal, the trophy, a win) becomes more important to you than the other people on the field or on your team, you will behave selfishly. Every time.

Selfishness means you'll spend most of your time asking questions like:

- What's in it for me?
- How many points/goals/touchdowns can I score?

- Will I be starting?
- Will I get the attention I deserve?
- Am I getting the most playing time?
- Will I be the MVP?[5]

These questions are about one person. ME. They are about making sure I get *my* due, that everyone sees *me* play, that *my* stats are the highest priority. All too often, this kind of selfishness is rewarded. It's encouraged by coaches, parents, and leagues, but that does not make it right. To be uncommon, selfish isn't good enough. We have to figure out how to play and live differently.

It's All About Pie

We know it's not good to be selfish. We've been told all our lives to share and be kind. We know it's a problem. But we cannot seem to stop the selfishness. And the reason, surprisingly, is *fear.*

Imagine you are in line to get a piece of pie. You watch as piece after piece is handed out, and suddenly, you're concerned. You start counting the people ahead of you. You tap your fork on your plate, hoping there's still some pie left when you get to the table, but you aren't really sure there's enough. So what happens?

When you get concerned enough, you will become selfish. You'll dive ahead. You'll push people out of the way. You will cut in line when they aren't looking. You will do whatever you can to get your slice of pie first and leave everyone else to divvy up what's left.[6]

Selfishness happens because you are afraid. Afraid there won't be enough to go around. Afraid your friend who's three spots in front of you is going to cut himself a giant slice of that pie, and you won't get any. It's fear of missing out that drives you to do selfish things, making everything about getting what you want and leaving everyone else out in the cold.

More Than Enough

We don't need to let fear drive us. We can choose not to be selfish, and it happens when we recognize there is actually more than enough to go around.

Despite what it feels like sometimes, success is not like a pie. Yes, there is one trophy, one championship game. But true success is not limited to the win-loss column. It's about more than who scores the most points. True success allows for winning, even when you lose. So instead of thinking in terms of one pie for everyone—a limited amount that can run out—we can choose to think of a bakery.

In a bakery, there is a lot of pie, many different kinds. More pies get made all the time. There is no limit. If that is true, I can relax. Since there is enough to go around, I can stop worrying about not getting my share, and when I'm no longer focused on getting my share, when I can believe that there is enough to go around, I can behave selflessly.

When you live out uncommon selflessness, you think about other people first. You think bigger than yourself. Because you know you'll be taken care of, you can give, instead of take. When you have uncommon selflessness, you ask questions like:

- How can I give to my teammates?
- How can I make those around me better?
- What can I do to help the team be successful?
- How can I contribute to this sport?
- How can I give to my opponents?[7]

Asking these questions will always get us to true success. They raise the bar and broaden your scope beyond your goals to the well-being of the other people involved. When you can ask these questions, you will be on the road to uncommon selflessness.

Me-first vs. Team-first

Selflessness comes from a trust that there will be enough. And the truth is, *there is*. There is enough success to go around, but still, it feels strange to give up our way. Aren't we supposed to go all-out for our own glory? Aren't we supposed to pursue our plans with passion? Isn't living selflessly going to take us farther away from our goals?

Actually, no.

Amazingly, when you start to lay down your personal goals for a bigger, other-centered approach, you will be more likely to achieve your personal goals. You will end up exactly where you were hoping to go, and for most athletes, that happens through their team.

Being on a team is one of the most rewarding aspects of sports. Working together toward a goal is an uncommon skill that will empower you to succeed in sports and in many other areas of life. Everyone has a team. Even if you don't play football or doubles tennis, you have a team. It may not be other people on the field with you. It can include parents, coaches, and fellow players. Everyone has a team.

Teamwork requires selflessness. You must learn to let the team be more important than yourself. In 2014, the Green Bay Packers needed to shake up their defense, so head coach Mike McCarthy asked Clay Matthews to switch positions. It would be a big change for him, but Matthews said he would try. He moved from a safe, familiar position where he'd excelled to a new, unfamiliar position for the team's benefit. And because he did, the team improved, winning five straight games.[8]

Clay Matthews put the needs of the team above his own comfort and accomplishments. He trusted that he didn't need to look out only for himself, and he gave up a position he was good at to help his team. Sadly, many athletes never learn to do this. Isaiah Thomas said, "It's hard to get people to overcome the thought that they have to take care of themselves first. It's hard to get players to give in to the group and become selfless as opposed to selfish."[9]

A selfish athlete will not give in to the team, and everyone around them will know. When "you're a selfish, attention-seeking show-boat, you will clearly communicate these qualities to all who are in your presence. In the process you will also turn off your teammates and coaches, disgust your opponents and demonstrate to the crowd that you are seriously lacking in character, style and class."[10] Obviously, this is not uncommon.

Giving in to the team is one of the most powerful strategies for success in sports. It means using your skills, not for self-glory, but for building up the team. And the greatest athletes in the world have learned that uncommon selflessness is the true path to greatness.

Michael Jordan was an incredible individual player, but even he had to learn to give to his teammates, worrying as much about their performances as his own. When he finally started to help them, the Bulls started winning championships.[11] Jordan said:

There are plenty of teams in every sport that have great players and never win titles. Most of the time, those players aren't willing to sacrifice for the greater good of the team. One thing I believe to the fullest is that if you think and achieve as a team, the individual accolades will take care of themselves. Talent wins games, but teamwork and intelligence win championships.[12]

The same is true for everyday players. At every level, there are players who refuse to seek glory and instead support the team. Basketball's sixth man is a great example. The sixth man is rarely a standout player. He doesn't start most games. He is not the player people pay to see. Instead, the sixth man comes off the bench during the game to play wherever he is most needed. He often covers more than one position; he is a master of offense and defense, and while many of today's players demand the spotlight, the sixth man wants the team to succeed more than he wants to be a star.

Like Mia Hamm, Michael Jordan and the sixth man, an uncommon athlete understands his true strength lies in sacrificing his own stats to make sure the team wins.

If you are a better, faster, stronger and more talented athlete than many of the other members on your squad, then your job, NO, your responsibility, is to help lift your teammates' level of play up another notch. It's up to you to inspire them and help them bring out their best. You do this by being supportive, positive, caring and forgiving. You do this by acting like and modeling being a champion.[13]

The uncommon athlete refuses to showboat to build her own reputation and focuses instead on helping her team. He encourages his teammates, works with them—in practice and in games—and understands that, when the team achieves great things, the individual always wins too.

It's Up To You

Whether you compete as an individual or on a team, in order to be uncommon, you must develop selflessness. No one can make you do it. It is your choice. A choice you have to make over and over until you develop a habit of selflessness. Let's break it down.

Choice #1: No Comparisons

One key to uncommon selflessness is comparison. Or, more accurately, choosing not to compare.

When we compare ourselves to our friends, our teammates, or our opponents, we will always lose. Other people are moving targets. They cannot be a solid foundation. Comparing ourselves to other people always results in self-doubt (because they seem better) or an ego trip (because we seem better). And neither view is helpful.

An uncommon athlete chooses not to compare. He knows he has strengths and weaknesses. He knows the other players do, too. She believes in her abilities, but recognizes that another player might also deserve recognition. Uncommon athletes do not measure their worth based on other people.

In 2012, Steph Curry signed a $44 million contract extension with the Golden State Warriors. In 2015, Curry led the team to an NBA Championship and was named League MVP. When Curry signed his contract extension, his future was uncertain. Now that he is one of the NBA's dominant players, his salary is well below what he is worth. But Curry chose not to compare. "I had to make a conscious decision and remind myself over and over [to let it go] ... You can't look back, because it'll bring negativity. It'll cause dissension in the team if you allow it to."[14]

Curry is not willing to risk the team and its goals over his pay. He does not sit around comparing his salary to the salaries of his teammates or his opponents. He simply plays, putting the team first.

Choice #2: Focus on the Positive
Uncommon selflessness chooses to see the positive in every situation.

This choice goes back to the pie illustration. It's all about perspective. When you see the world as a single pie that you have to get your share of, you will quickly fall into selfish behaviors. You will cut others down. You will focus on your own success. You cannot see the world negatively and behave selflessly.

So uncommon athletes choose to be positive. They practice gratitude. They know the "bakery" isn't going to run out of pie, so they relax and do their best. They realize they've already enjoyed a huge share of pie (things like talent, attention, playing time), so they don't have to run around trying to grab it from other people. Instead, they are willing to share what they do have.

Focusing on the positive means having a good attitude. If pushed, many athletes will give up their way, but they do it grudgingly and with a bad attitude. Choosing selflessness means giving up your way and doing it cheerfully, even gratefully.

When asked about his salary, Steph Curry said, "I've tried to just be appreciative of what I have. I'm taken care of, and I'm thankful that I can be on the court able to play at a high level. I'm thankful it's not the other way around, that I didn't become an overpaid player. That's a different conversation."[15]

Selflessness means we keep our focus on our goals instead of ourselves and choose to be grateful even when life, or the game, or the referee's call doesn't go our way.

Choice #3: Protect Others

This choice is about humility. Humility is the choice to *not* be proud. It is choosing to be modest and teachable, *not* arrogant or conceited.[16] Humility shows up most clearly in how we treat other people.

An uncommon athlete will always look out for others first. She responds to people with respect and kindness. He doesn't taunt or bully. However humility is more than simply *not* putting someone down or *not* treating the JV team badly. It means actively treating others well. It's about being the one who protects.

We will always protect what is important to us. We lock our house when we leave it. We chain our bike to the bike rack. We save our money in a bank (piggy or otherwise). But uncommon selflessness sees the value of people, too. It's choosing not to worry about yourself–your position, your popularity, your reputation–and instead, looking for ways you can protect others. It's a choice to intentionally build up a younger player or actively protect someone who's being bullied.[17] It's taking time out of your day to take care of someone else.

FSU football player Travis Rudolph is a great example of this. While the Florida State players were visiting Montford Middle School, they joined the students for lunch. Rudolph saw a boy eating alone and asked to sit with him. The boy, who has Autism, often eats alone, but on that day, Rudolph made sure he did not. It wasn't a publicity stunt; he simply reached out to a young man sitting alone. It was selfless.[18]

Teams can show this selflessness, too. When a man in their town was injured in a motorcycle accident, eventually losing part of his leg, the Buckhorn Bucks football team stepped in to help the family. On a Saturday morning, they showed up to do yard work, meeting a need the family couldn't manage on their own. They could have slept in or done a morning practice. Instead, they put someone else's needs above their own. They protected their neighbor.[19]

Like Travis Rudolph and the Bucks football team, be the one who protects. Protect your team, your teammates, your coach and your school. Protect them physically. Protect their reputations. Be the one who fights for those who cannot fight for themselves. It is selfless, and it always brings honor.[20]

Choice #4: Do the Right Thing

Uncommon selflessness means that you don't ever cheat or lie to win. Ever. It means doing the right thing is more important than your own success. Yes, it can be humiliating to tell the truth. Mistakes can be costly, and small errors sometimes cost you the game. It's easier to hide them, but it's also selfish. And it's never uncommon.

In 2005, Andy Roddick was one point from a win at the Rome Masters tournament. His opponent missed his first serve, and then his second. The umpire started to award Roddick the match, but Roddick stopped him. He pointed out that the second ball had been in. After checking, the line judge changed the call, and play continued. Roddick eventually lost the match and the tournament.

A selfish choice would have been understandable. Roddick could have said nothing and taken home the trophy. No one would have even known about the line judge's error, but Roddick choose to be selfless. He was uncommon, and though his honesty cost him the match, it gave him a much more important win.[21]

Uncommon athletes know that doing the right thing is always the most important thing. When you play your game, be a truth-teller. Own up to your mistakes, even if it costs you. Never lie to your coach, the ump, or your team. Be a good sport. Honor your teammates and your opponents above your own achievements. Play respectfully and according to the rules. Play to win, but be willing to empower others, even as you do your very best.

A Hard Road

Uncommon selflessness is not the norm. The overall culture of sports in our country does not encourage it. It is not expected. It is rarely rewarded, and it is not easy. Being selfless might mean somebody could take advantage of you. It might mean giving up a position or a play that you really wanted to have, but it is worth it. Because those concerns are short-term problems. You cannot sacrifice being uncommon for a short-term win.

Living selflessly always leads to a life of greater significance. Selfless athletes play for their teammates. They give great effort and play with great spirit so they don't let down their team. This commitment to making others better, while sometimes costly in the short-run, makes for richer relationships, stronger teams and greater victories in the long run. And that is uncommon.

TALK About It

1. Do you think living selflessly is really worth the cost? Why or why not?

2. List three ways a team might behave selfishly. Now list three ways your team can display uncommon selflessness.

3. Do you compare yourself to other people? What happens when you do?

4. Why is gratitude so important? How can you practice being more thankful?

5. It's easy to want to put ourselves first, but what would it look like for you, or your team, to make protecting each other a priority?

Chapter 5

UNCOMMON INTEGRITY

Integrity is a trait we're all capable of having–and should have–but manifesting it daily is the test we're graded on … forever

A Half-Million Dollar Mistake

In 2010, Jeremy Affeldt, relief pitcher for the San Francisco Giants, signed a $10 million contract extension, but an error in the contract meant the Giants organization was paying him an extra $500,000, on top of his actual salary. When he realized the error, Affeldt got a number of opinions on what he should do. Legally, everyone said, the money was his to keep.

Affeldt gave it back. After discussing the unintended bonus with his agent and with the Giants, Affeldt had the contract rewritten to fix the error. He told them, "I can't take that money. I won't sleep well at night knowing I took that money because every time I open my paycheck I'll know it's not right."[1]

Jeremy Affeldt showed uncommon integrity. When he realized the contract was incorrect, he revealed it instead of hiding it. When he could have kept the money, he gave it back. Instead of helping himself at the expense of the team, he chose to abide by their original agreement. In other words, he did the right thing.

The Puzzle of You

Integrity is "a firm adherence to a code, the quality or state of being undivided."[2] It's really about character. Integrity requires that what you say and what you do align. If you say you believe something, you live that way. If you claim to be against something, you don't do it when no one's watching. The bottom-line question integrity asks is: does your life match?

Another way to think about integrity is wholeness. Having integrity means you can't live from only parts of your heart, or only with your brain and not your heart. A person with integrity is a whole person and whole athlete. He is complete.

So how does integrity happen? Think of it like putting together a puzzle of your life. It comes in pieces in a box with a picture on the front, a picture of the real you. As we go through life, we're putting the pieces together for everyone else to see. When a person lacks integrity, the puzzle is left unfinished. Pieces are missing, or they are jammed into the puzzle in all the wrong places. They are included, but the picture is all messed up.

Sometimes a lack of integrity means all the pieces are put together, but the picture doesn't match the one on the box. In real life, that means pretending to be something we're not. We wear a mask so that we look like someone else, or what someone else wants us to look like. But it's not us. It's not who we really are. Our puzzle is done, but it's not complete.

It is possible to put your puzzle together with integrity. There are no missing pieces. The pieces are all put into the correct spots. The picture matches the box, and it's the real you. Not a version of you that you pretend to be. You are whole. You are complete. That is integrity, and that is a fundamental part of being an uncommon athlete.

Part I: Behavior
Uncommon Integrity always affects how you behave. When your life matches the principles you say you believe, you will live well.

First, you will live honestly.[3] You won't lie. You won't cheat. You won't behave one way in school but the opposite when you're out with friends. There is no deceit, no deception. What you see is what you get, and there is no double-ness to your life.

Second, you will live rightly.[4] This kind of life means you do the right thing. You act justly. You are fair. In this sense, integrity means your life is the opposite of wicked. Instead of bullying, you are kind. Instead of flippant, you are careful. Instead of lazy, you are diligent. That is living with integrity.

This kind of life is powerful. Like wearing a seatbelt in a car or wearing protective gear during competition, maintaining uncommon integrity keeps you safe. It keeps your life from collapsing around you. Some athletes take this truth seriously, and they choose their actions and words carefully. Every day, however, we see the stories of athletes who are living without integrity plastered all over sports blogs and ESPN. No matter how they try to hide their lack of integrity, they are always, eventually, discovered.[5]

Lance Armstrong learned this lesson the hard way. For over a decade, Armstrong denied taking performance enhancing drugs. When he finally admitted to doping, he lost his integrity, his reputation and all of his Tour de France titles. Even the foundation he created cut its ties with him. As Armstrong found out, integrity is not about what you say, but what you do ... or don't do.

It is possible to find athletes with uncommon integrity. Some athletes choose to do the right thing, even when no one is watching and even if it costs them the game or the record.

High school senior Nate Hassis was just 29 yards shy of the conference passing-yard record, with 30 seconds left in his final game, when his coach called a time-out to talk with their opponents. When play resumed, it was clear the coaches had "arranged" for Hassis to break the record. His final pass went to a wide-open receiver who ran 37 yards, giving him the record. Except it didn't. Hassis refused to accept a record that wasn't won fairly and asked that the pass be removed from his stats.[6] That is uncommon integrity.

Part II: Reputation

Uncommon integrity affects more than your behavior, however. It is also the foundation for a good reputation.

Your reputation is what comes to someone's mind when they think about you. Good or bad, every person is known for being a certain way, and it only takes the mention of his or her name to bring that reputation to mind.[7] Your reputation is important, but not because of other people's opinions. It's important because it is the most valuable asset you have. More than superior stats and high-profile contracts, an uncommon athlete knows that "a good name is more desirable than great riches."[8] It is worth more than gold.

One of the best examples is David Robinson.

Nicknamed "The Admiral" during his time at the Naval Academy, Robinson was a stand-out center for the San Antonio Spurs. He was league MVP in 1995, won two championships with the Spurs in 1999 and 2003, and won Olympic gold medals in 1992 and 1996. During his 14-year career, Robinson was admired on the court for his formidable skills and off the court for his commitment to his team and his community, even winning the

2003 Sports Illustrated Sportsperson of the Year award.[9]

While Robinson worked hard to be the best on the court and in life, he always understood the value of a good reputation. "What I need to do is have a great positive attitude and a great work ethic. Those two things validate me. Yes, it's important that I have good numbers, and I'm well-respected as a player, but I think it's more important that I'm respected as a man."[10]

Uncommon integrity is about more than just an athlete's game-time performance. Integrity requires wholeness in *every* aspect of life. David Robinson is a great example of this, too.

On the court, Robinson regularly posted high stats in scoring, rebounding and blocked shots. He also worked hard to be a team player. Drafted by the Spurs in 1987, he fulfilled his two-year commitment to the Navy before joining the team and then played his entire career for the Spurs. He always put the team first. He said, "I think any player will tell you that individual accomplishments help your ego, but ... it counts more that the team has played well."[11] When the Spurs drafted Tim Duncan in 1997, Robinson willingly gave up the spotlight, helping to mentor Duncan even as he continued to play his best.

Robinson's integrity was apparent in his reputation off the court, as well. He is known for being kind and attentive to players, fans and the media. He has a solid family and prepared ahead for life after basketball. He has contributed so powerfully to the community of San Antonio that the winner of the NBA Community Assist Award now receives the David Robinson plaque. He even created a non-profit organization to assist other celebrities with their charitable investments. He gives back, and he helps others do it, too.[12]

David Robinson's life and career are unsullied by bad press, bad decisions or personal misconduct. He was elected to the Hall of Fame in 2005, and in his speech he praised his sons and wife, thanked his family and the Spurs organization, and thanked the audience for coming to share that moment with him.[13] His humility, grace and consideration of others made him great, on and off the court. He is the perfect example of uncommon integrity.

A Delicate Thread

Unfortunately, uncommon integrity is rare. For every David Robinson, we could easily name twenty athletes who lost their integrity (or never had it to begin with). Integrity takes a lifetime to build but only a moment to erase.

Think about Tiger Woods. For years, he was the reigning king of professional golf. He was respected and believed in; fans loved him. Then, his integrity took a major hit. Despite his squeaky clean image, claims that he had cheated on his wife damaged his reputation, and since he's no longer winning as handily as he once did, his reputation is no longer positive in the public's mind.[14]

An uncommon reputation is incredibly fragile. It's that perfect, expensive, breakable vase that your mom keeps on the highest shelf. You aren't allowed to even run past it, for fear it will tip off and shatter. Your integrity is just as breakable as that vase. Only you can protect it. Like an offensive lineman has to move, watch, and sacrifice for the quarterback he is protecting, uncommon integrity must be actively guarded. There are two simple principles that will help you protect your reputation: *Think* and *Wait*.[15]

Before you make a choice. Before you do anything. *Think* about it. Ask yourself questions about the choice. Is it wise? Will doing it hurt you? Will it hurt someone else? What might happen as a result of this decision? *Think* about what you're doing. And then, *wait* before you act. Nothing worth doing has to be done *right.this.second*. If someone is pressuring you, telling you how urgent it is for you to decide, back away. Give it an hour. Give it a day. Give yourself time to get some perspective so you can make a wise decision and protect your integrity.

Your reputation will be remembered long after you are gone. It is a lifetime investment. Make it your highest goal to be remembered well. It's fine to want your number retired. It's great to pursue sports at the next level. If your reputation is ruined, though, if you lose your integrity, none of what you accomplish will matter. Do everything you can to be the kind of person that others want to be like. Like David Robinson...make uncommon integrity your highest priority.

The Influence of Integrity

To be uncommon, you have to maintain your integrity every day at practice, in competition, and in life. Although it is a difficult path, it is also an inspiring and powerful way to live. Even if doing the right thing sometimes costs you, it gives you great influence.

Influence is the ability to affect other people, and it can be good or bad. But with uncommon integrity, you will be able to influence others in good ways. Your coach, your team and others in your life will trust that you say what you mean and do what you say. Because they trust you, they'll follow you. You'll be able to encourage them to stay on the uncommon path, and you can speak up when they are tempted to step toward lesser things.

This influence will be most evident with your teammates. An

uncommon athlete doesn't just live with integrity; she also requires integrity from her team. He chooses to live honestly and rightly, which means he will not stand by while his teammates choose to live the opposite.

First, he will not stand by while his teammates display ... a *poor work ethic*. Living rightly always means giving your all, in the game, in practice and in life. Uncommon athletes prepare and play with integrity. They "work hard or go home." They are always willing to go the extra mile in practice and in the game, and they expect their teammates to do the same. They will speak against laziness. They will encourage those who are struggling, but they will never allow the team to be unwilling to work hard.

She will also not stand for ... *excuses*. An uncommon athlete refuses to give excuses, and she won't hear them from her teammates. Integrity is about wholeness. Values match behavior. So if the team's mantra is "fight hard," the uncommon athlete will hold her team to it. She'll make sure her behavior matches what she says she will do, and she'll encourage the rest of the team to do the same. Playing with integrity means finding a way to get the job done ... as a team ... no excuses.

Lastly, an uncommon athlete will never tolerate ... *disrespect*. Uncommon athletes won't be disrespectful to the coaches or refs, and they will not allow their teammates to behave that way either. That's not all. Uncommon athletes will also stand against any player who misrepresents the program or the team on the field, in the classroom and in the community. In the movie *Remember the Titans*, Gerry Bertier, one of the white players on the team, asks the coach to cut his friend, Ray, even though the coach has a no-cut policy. He tells Coach Boone, "I know that Ray missed that block on purpose. Sometimes you just got to cut a man loose." Ray's bad attitude and his refusal to play his position well caused the quarterback's injury and hurt the team, on the field and in the community. Bertier wouldn't allow his friend that level of negative influence. He expected integrity on his team, and he was willing to bear the responsibility of cutting his friend to see the team stay whole.[16]

Uncommon Integrity

Integrity requires wholehearted living. Everything you do, for your entire life, works together to build your reputation, on and off the field. One mistake can undo that reputation in a heartbeat. It is up to you to protect your integrity, making choices that build value into your name so you can create a positive and powerful influence on those around you. No game, no hobby, no boyfriend or girlfriend, no Friday night "fun" is worth permanently damaging your name. Make uncommon integrity your goal.

TALK About It

1. Think again about Jeremy Affeldt. If you were in his shoes, would you have given the money back?

2. Why is integrity so important? What would life be like if no one had integrity?

3. Describe what it means to "live honestly" and "live rightly" in your own words.

4. Why is a reputation so easily destroyed? How can "think and wait" help you protect your reputation and your integrity?

5. Do you think one player with integrity can really influence the whole team? What other negatives (like poor work ethic, excuses,

and disrespect) might be addressed by a team leader (or leaders) who want to live and play with integrity?

Chapter 6

UNCOMMON OVERCOMING

The next level of success never requires you to go under; superior achievement always forces you to overcome.

A Part of Life

An uncommon athlete displays all the hallmarks of PASSION, but having PASSION does not mean your life is smooth sailing. No matter how well you're doing, no matter your level of success, you will eventually face a major obstacle.

Obstacles are part of everyone's game plan, whether they want them or not. So you must take them into account. You have to plan for them, even if you don't know exactly when they will come or what they will look like. When you expect them, you will be more ready to respond appropriately.

When she was four years old, Wilma Rudolph contracted polio, and the disease left her with a twisted leg and foot. The doctors told her she would never walk again, but she did. She walked with a brace, enduring years of therapy, until finally, she was able to compete as a teenager. She was truly an overcomer. Even more, she was a champion. She became the fastest woman in the world, winning three gold medals in the 1960 Olympic games – the first woman ever to manage that feat![1]

Years later, Rudolph said, "Nobody goes undefeated all the time. If you can pick up after a crushing defeat, and go on to win again, you are going to be a champion someday."[2] Whether that defeat comes from an opponent or an obstacle, no athlete is automatically out of the running. Rudolph worked hard to overcome, and every uncommon athlete can do the same.

Observing Obstacles

An obstacle is "something that stands in the way or opposes; something that hinders progress."[3] It's a glitch, a barrier, a snag. It is any*thing* or any*one* who keeps you from reaching your goal. Obstacles are not easy to face. They are real. They are hard. They hurt, if you aren't prepared for them, they will bench you, at least for a while.

For many athletes, circumstances are obstacles. It might be an injury, a physical or mental or emotional condition you have to deal with. It might be a car wreck, a mental block, a personal or family crisis. You might fail a class and get cut from the team. You might come in fifth in a race you needed to win. These are all obstacles.

Tamika Catchings's challenge is a disability. She is a fifteen-year veteran of the WNBA. She was the League MVP in 2011 and the Finals MVP in 2012. She has four Olympic gold medals.[4] Catchings was also born with a hearing disability that affected both ears. As a child, she was teased over her hearing aids and speech impediment, and she struggled with being different. She has worked to overcome this roadblock all her life.[5]

Obstacles can also be people, girlfriend or boyfriend who distracts you or a friend who talks trash. A new coach who benches you or an opponent who finishes two seconds faster than you in every race. Sometimes it is other people who can keep us from our goals. The doctors were Wilma Rudolph's obstacle. They looked at her injury and told her not to even try. They said her situation was hopeless, and she had lost the chance to walk. That kind of negative talk, from friends or experts, can be a major roadblock for any athlete who wants desperately to reach her goals.

Sometimes, the obstacle is simply life. You're tired. You're busy. Your family moves every ten or fifteen months. You struggle to balance school and sports, friends and family, so you never seem to be able to make progress toward your goals. Life became an obstacle for Elena Delle Donne. A WNBA MVP and Olympic gold medalist, she actually quit basketball after high school because of burnout. She had poured her whole life into her game, but suddenly, playing was the last thing she wanted to do. The schedule and training wore her out, and the thing she loved most became her roadblock.[6]

Obstacles are very real, and they are hard to face. It will hurt when they crash into your life and mess up your dreams, but it is possible to overcome.

The Key is Attitude
Sadly, many athletes do not become uncommon overcomers. They face an obstacle, and it completely derails them. The injury ends their career. The mental block keeps them from going pro. Their personal drama crushes them until they fall apart, on the field and in life. But an uncommon athlete will fight to get over, around, or through the obstacle. They get moving, keep moving, and stay confident until they find a way to conquer their mountain. As William Arthur Ward put it, "Adversity causes some men to break; others to break records."[7]

So what is the difference? Why do some athletes become overcomers, and others do not? The key is *attitude.*

Your outlook will always determine your outcome. Every time.

Not because a positive attitude makes everything go your way. This is not about "good karma" or whether you can cause good things to happen to you by thinking happy thoughts. Having the attitude of an uncommon overcomer means you look ahead to the goal you want to reach and keep going toward it, no matter what.

And to develop this attitude, an uncommon athlete will change their perspective, avoid the pitfalls and stay proactive. Let's look at each one.

Change Your Perspective

When an obstacle crashes into your life, your instinct will be to focus entirely on that roadblock. If you aren't careful, you can feel as if you are suffocating under its weight. But keeping an Uncommon perspective will help you deal with whatever is keeping you from your goal.

1. Keep it broad

In the face of a major obstacle, an uncommon athlete refuses to become narrow-minded. Like a wide-angle lens on a camera, having a broad focus helps you to put your obstacle in context. It is part of your life, but it is only one part of it. Yes, a torn ACL will put you on the bench, but your family life, your school work and your friendships haven't changed. Remind yourself that most of your life is in good shape. Repeat the truth that this one issue does not negate every other area of life. Enlist others to remind you of this often, even as you work to overcome the roadblock in your way.

2. Keep it long-term.

Focusing only on the obstacle itself also traps us in the sadness of our current situation. Obstacles hurt. We are afraid we'll never get past it. We wonder if we'll ever reach our goal, but choosing the long-term view will prevent you from drowning in the emotions of the moment. You will find hope. Bob Feller said, "Every day is a new opportunity. You can build on yesterday's success or put its failures behind and start over again. That's the way life is, with a new game every day, and that's the way baseball is."[8] Stay committed to the goals you have set. Your path may look different, you may have to adjust, but you can still get there. Today's problems do not doom you to a life of failure. One obstacle does not erase the future's possibilities. Keep the long-term view.[9]

3. Keep it positive.

An uncommon overcomer looks at his or her situation and chooses to see the good. She focuses on the blessings, the highlights of her life, not just the hardships. He knows staying positive will give an internal power that negativity cannot provide. As coach Pat Riley once said, "If you have a positive attitude and constantly strive to give your best effort, eventually you will overcome your immediate problems and find you are ready for greater challenges.[10]

Avoid the Pitfalls

Trying to find a way around or through an obstacle can sometimes feel like navigating a minefield. Every few steps, you seem to run into another danger. These three choices will help you avoid some of the most common pitfalls that can trip you up as you work to overcome.

1. Ask what, not why.

When you demand to know the reason for a roadblock, you will get stuck. You will never move past it. Wondering "why" you've gotten injured or been benched is fine for a moment, but eventually, you have to set that aside so you can continue to move forward. The truth is, life rarely gives us the "why" we desperately want. We may never know why something happened to us, but we can continue to deal with it. And to do that, we must change our question to "what."

- What can I do to respond to this problem?
- What is something good that's come from this situation?
- What am I feeling about this problem?
- What can I learn from this obstacle?

By developing the habit of asking "what" instead of "why," we can continue to move forward instead of getting swallowed up in self-pity.[11]

2. Avoid Blame

We blame others to push our pain onto someone else. If it's their fault, then maybe it won't hurt so badly. Blaming is normal. When we are dealing with an obstacle, there is a lot of hurt. Our plan has been derailed. The goal suddenly seems far away. So we blame. We blame the opponent. We blame the coach. We blame the weather, our parents or our teammates.

But an uncommon athlete must be very careful with blame. While it's normal to feel hurt by a sudden obstacle, it is never okay to hurt others in response. Especially when they are, most likely, not the real problem. Even worse, blame undermines our accountability. The more we blame, the less responsibility we take to solve the problem. We say, "It's someone else's fault, so it's someone else's problem," but life doesn't work that way.[12]

An obstacle is never an excuse to push off our frustration onto someone else. Even when someone else was at fault (say you are injured in a car accident with a drunk driver), nothing is solved by blame. Instead, you have to choose not to be a victim and take responsibility for what you actually can control, no matter how small that may be. That choice to avoid blame will put you on the road toward restoring your dreams. It's how you overcome.

3. Don't lose faith.

Our obstacles are the testing ground not just for our athletic dreams, but for our character and our personal growth. An uncommon athlete is never content to develop speed, skill and stamina on the field without also developing maturity and leadership off the field.

Often, it is in facing obstacles that our maturity and character are formed.[13] In those moments, we have to hold tightly to the faith we have: in other people, in God and in ourselves. When a roadblock comes, it is tempting to believe the worst, to wonder if God still cares and to doubt our own ability.

However faith means trust. Trust that things will turn out, even though events have not.[14] As Warren Wiersbe said, "God doesn't always change the circumstances, but He can change us to meet the circumstances. That's what it means to live by faith."[15]

Get Moving

Finally, when obstacles come, the single most important thing you can do is simply start moving forward again. W. Clement Stone said, "Thinking will not overcome fear, but action will."[16]

In 1925, Gertrude Ederle attempted to swim the English Channel. Swimming the Channel is extremely hard. It requires a swim of at least 21 miles, in freezing cold water, fighting the tide and jellyfish. Ederle was determined to become the first woman to make it across, but her coach doubted her ability to finish. Despite all of her hard work, he insisted that she quit after almost nine hours in the water.

It was a major setback for Ederle, but she chose to keep moving. Within months, Ederle found a new coach and continued her training, and in August 1926, she completed her Channel swim in 14 1/2 hours, two hours faster than the previous record. Ederle refused to be undone by people, circumstances, or her own doubts. And she accomplished a feat that no woman, and few men before her had.[17]

The best way to respond to any roadblock in your path is to keep moving, however you can. Take small steps. Rehab that injury. Watch game tapes. Come to practice and team meetings even if you can't play. No matter what you "can't" do, you can choose to keep moving, and those small action steps will eventually build the momentum you need to keep pursuing your original goal.

Building Bridges

When you become an uncommon overcomer, you will know you can face any obstacle that comes, but facing and overcoming obstacles is never about pride; it's about connection. It's not about feeding your ego. Instead, overcoming helps you develop empathy so you can help other athletes who are also struggling. Overcoming is not about proving you are superhuman, but it is a powerful path toward becoming truly human.

Team Hoyt is a great example of this. Dick Hoyt and his son, Rick, are long-distance competitors who run races together. But They are a very unique team. Rick Hoyt was born with cerebral palsy. He is wheelchair-bound and uses a special computer to communicate, but when he was 15, he told his dad he wanted to participate in a charity race. So his dad pushed him in the race, and Team Hoyt was born. Rick told his dad, "When I'm running, it feels like I'm not handicapped."

Since that race in 1977, father and son have run over 1,000

marathons, distance races, and triathlons together. They've even completed 6 ironman competitions and the Boston Marathon thirty-two times. For most of their running career, they competed in up to 50 races each year, though now they've cut back to only 20-25. In every race, the Hoyts' goal was always to finish well, and they have.[18]

Things have not been easy for Team Hoyt. They have faced and overcome uncountable obstacles along the way. The races themselves were grueling. Rick's medical issues required specialized equipment. In some cases, they were not allowed to compete at all. Despite the challenges, they kept lining up. They kept running, and because they did, they have inspired millions.

Overcoming unites people. Team Hoyt's obstacles were what connected them to other athletes, other families and other people living with disabilities. By overcoming, they gained hundreds of opportunities to share their story and encourage others to overcome their obstacles as well.

Overcoming Obstacles

In sports and in life, we rarely get the opportunity of a "do over." Life doesn't come with pause or reset buttons, and we cannot DVR a game or an opportunity to save it for later, but we always have the chance to overcome. Our challenge is to live today, keeping our focus on the end goal, while we work to overcome whatever obstacles we face.

For Tamika Catchings, sports provided an opportunity to define herself by how hard she worked, instead of by her disability. Despite her hearing impairment, she has excelled in sports and in life, giving back to her community and turning every difficulty into another possibility to do something great.[19]

Elena Delle Donne dealt with her burnout by taking a year away from basketball. She played volleyball, hoping to compete at the Olympics in that sport instead, but after a year away, she picked up a basketball again and knew she had come home. Her passion was back, and she pursued her sport again with pleasure.[20]

An athlete is not uncommon because he never runs into hard things. He becomes uncommon because, when faced with hard things, he refuses to stop until he has overcome. Michael Jordan said, "If you're trying to achieve there will be roadblocks. I've had them; everybody has had them. But obstacles don't have to stop you. If you run into a wall, don't turn around and give up. Figure out how to climb it, go through it, or work around it."[21]

Be an uncommon overcomer.

TALK About It

1. Do you know of anyone who has faced major obstacles, in sports or in life? How did he or she overcome those obstacles?

2. Which of the pitfalls (asking why, blaming others, losing faith) are you most likely to fall into? What can you do to avoid that response the next time an obstacle comes?

3. Why is being proactive–getting moving again–an important step in uncommon overcoming?

4. Overcoming is something we have to do in all of life. In what specific areas outside of athletics do you need to develop an attitude of overcoming?

5. Team Hoyt formed when a dad helped his son overcome his

disability and run in a race, and they have inspired millions with their story. How can you help someone else become an overcomer?

Chapter 7

UNCOMMON NERVE

*Dissect the nerves of a champion, and you're sure to find courage,
spirit, and truth, affirmed with a boldness
of faith – how can they lose?*

It's All About Nerve

The last hallmark of PASSION is uncommon nerve. In the face
of trials or obstacles, nerve is what helps you move forward.
When you are going through the weeks, months or years of
preparation, it is nerve that keeps you fighting through each day.
Nerve is absolutely necessary. You will never achieve true success
without it.

Uncommon nerve is best seen when the pressure is on, when an
athlete comes to a crisis moment. It all comes down to a single
play, a single race, a single routine, and somehow he or she rises
to the challenge. Nerve is Kerri Strug's second vault on an injured
ankle in the 1996 Olympic games. It is Derek Redmond crossing
the finish line with his dad after injuring his hamstring in the 1994
Olympics. In the 2016 Olympics, it was was Jeffrey Julmis, a
Haitian hurdler who tripped on the first hurdle in his semifinal
heat. But he collected himself and kept going. He completed his
race, even though he had no chance to place.[1]

Nerve is the iron will to keep going when everything goes wrong,
when a single mistake seems to cost you everything, when injury
threatens to stop you cold. Uncommon nerve is the attitude that
never gives up. It *never.gives.up.* An uncommon athlete sets her
sights high and keeps going, no matter what. He pursues his goals
without reserve. He holds nothing back. Uncommon athletes

have the determination and drive to get exactly where they want to go. That is nerve.

Adjustment AND Nerve?

But what about adjustment? In chapter 2, we saw that an Uncommon athlete is flexible and can change course, finding a Plan B when necessary. That sounds like the opposite of nerve, doesn't it? Can "be flexible" and "never give up" somehow work together?

The answer is yes. Adjustment is not the opposite of nerve. Instead, they are two sides of the same coin. To get where you want to go, you will need both flexibility (an attitude of adjustment) and nerve.

The ultimate goal for an uncommon athlete is always true success, to reach your goals and achieve a wholehearted life. However, obstacles, other players, injuries or a D in Chemistry can rise up to keep you from success. At some point, you will have to bend. You will have to change course. You will have to reset your plans and try something new.

Plan B only works, though, if you also have the nerve to keep moving forward. It is easy to get off track when we change course. If we aren't careful, we can get stuck making adjustments, or focusing on the details, and we forget to get back to actually pursuing our goals. Adjustment moves us around the roadblock. Nerve is what gets us back in the field again. To be uncommon, we need them both.

Fear: Nerve's True Archenemy

Like every superhero has a nemesis (think Superman and Lex Luthor), uncommon nerve does have an opposite. There is a force you will have to defeat over and over again to develop nerve, and it isn't flexibility.

The opposite of uncommon nerve is *fear*.

In life and in sports, we face big challenges, and in the moment we dig down for nerve, we often find fear first. We are tired. We are discouraged. We have run out of energy and patience and strength. So we find ourselves afraid. Afraid we won't be enough. Afraid the other team will be better than us. Afraid we won't really be able to do what must be done.

This kind of fear can paralyze us unless we can figure out how to shake off its icy grip and get moving again.

Sometimes, this means breaking through fear. It's knuckling down and pushing through. To feel the fear and let it push you toward your goal. As Nelson Mandela said, "The brave man is not he who does not feel afraid, but he who conquers that fear."[2] Sometimes our fear can actually drive us forward.

We can't always power through, though. Sometimes, we have to face fear. Redirect it. At times, we need practical strategies to help us move past fear to nerve. Here are four.

First, you can *outthink* fear. Jack Nicklaus said, "Concentration is a fine antidote to anxiety."[3] When you're afraid, your emotions are running the show. So you have to turn your brain back on. Think out loud about the situation. Name the problem. Name your fear. Make yourself be logical and rational to bring your emotions back in check.

Second, you can *un-think* fear. Instead of thinking more about fear, you distract yourself. Watch a funny movie. Call a friend and chat. Go back to the basics of your sport. Do drills. Find a small, repetitive move that will help you get into a zone where fear cannot come and that will remind you that you do have the skills to play your game well.

Third, you can *imagine* your fear. Imagine what would happen if your fear came true. Imagine it all the way out to the last possible end result (which is what you really fear most of all). Surprisingly, this technique helps you realize that your worst possible fear is very, very unlikely. It shrinks your fear down to a manageable size so you can deal with it.

Last, you can *release* it. Praying can help you let go of fear.[4] Breathing patterns and visualizations can be good options. Listening to a playlist that psyches you up for competition can also be an effective response (think Michael Phelps's warrior face during the Rio Olympics). Find a go-to technique that will help you release your fear so you can perform at your very best.

Fear will keep you from your goal if you let it, but you can defeat fear. You can find nerve, and it starts in your mind.

It's All in your Mind

Attitude is important for an uncommon athlete, but attitude is not enough when it comes to nerve.

Nerve cannot come from performance or popularity. It will not come from other people's approval. Uncommon nerve has to come from deep inside you. It's not just wishful thinking. It's not visualizations. The foundation of uncommon nerve is what you think, whether you are convinced you can reach your goal or your team is ready to rise to the challenge. As Jack Nicklaus said, "Sometimes the biggest problem is in your head. You've got to believe you can play a shot instead of wondering where your next bad shot is coming from."[5]

Nerve is always dependent on what you believe, deep inside. If you do not believe you can reach your goal, you won't. "An unwavering belief must lead the way or else all the other efforts will be futile."[6] Uncommon nerve is a mindset based on two key truths, truths about who you are and about what you're doing.

Truth #1 "I am enough."
The key word is confidence. Nerve comes when you no longer have anything to prove. When you are confident you can rise to the challenge and accomplish what you set out to do. You know your strengths and weaknesses, you've worked hard to prepare, and you realize that win or lose, you are already a champion. This confidence is part of the uncommon life. When you are uncommon, you are complete. You are enough. You don't have to win another game or score another point. The critics don't weigh you down and the groupies don't swell your ego. You are enough just as you are, and because you're enough, you can confidently go out and play or run or swim or jump. You can keep going, trusting you'll find the nerve you need.

Truth #2 "This is worth it."
The key word here is motivation. Nerve comes from knowing you are doing exactly what you're supposed to do. Someone once said, "When you feel like quitting, think about why you started." That "why" is your motivation. Nerve is never about approval or attention. Instead, nerve comes from a love for the game, the joy of being on the field, the fulfillment of being part of a team. Mia Hamm said, "Somewhere behind the athlete you've become and

the hours of practice and the coaches who have pushed you is a little girl who fell in love with the game and never looked back ... play for her."[7] When you keep your focus on what motivated you from the start, you will always have the nerve to play the game well.

Nerve starts in the mind. An uncommon athlete believes in himself. She believes she can keep going, come back tomorrow, do better next time. So she does. Uncommon athletes become great because they are certain that they can be great. As Alabama head coach Paul "Bear" Bryant said, "If you believe in yourself, have dedication and pride–and never quit, you'll be a winner."[8]

Getting To It

The foundation is not enough all by itself, though. We have to put that foundation into action. We've already said that nerve is refusing to give up. It's the athlete who keeps going, no matter what. It's a deep down confidence and motivation that fuels you when the pressure is on.

In real life, in the middle of the game, what does nerve actually look like? How does it play out when the game is on the line? Uncommon nerve always displays four key qualities.

Nerve is Determination

Uncommon nerve means you have an internal drive to go forward. You are purposeful, even stubborn. With an absolute belief in yourself and your ability to succeed, you push toward your goals. There is no halfway. There is no maybe. It's an unflinching determination to achieve great things.

Michael Redd displayed this determination when he blew his left knee. He was at the top of his game. He'd finished the best season of his career and won gold in the 2008 Olympics, but in January of 2009, he tore both his ACL and MCL. It was a major injury that ended his season. After months in rehab, Redd returned to start the next fall. He was determined to play again, and he did.

Then the unexpected happened. Almost exactly one year after his injury, in January 2010, he was injured again. Same knee, same damage. With both ligaments torn in the same leg, his season ended early for a second year in a row. Many said he would never come back, and for most athletes, a second comeback from such a major injury would be impossible.

However, Michael Redd had uncommon nerve. He was determined to play in the NBA again. After 14 months in rehab, he returned to the Bucks in March 2011, completing the season without further injury. Michael Redd played the following year for the Phoenix Suns before retiring from the NBA. His determination had paid off. He retired a champion.[9]

Determination means you don't give excuses, and you never stop trying. You adjust your plan and keep going. You implement new drills or techniques to improve. No matter what, you persevere and make it through.

Nerve is No Retreat
Uncommon nerve is more than a determination to go forward. It also means refusing to retreat. Uncommon athletes do not back down; they do not turn tail and run. Like a general who burns the bridges behind his troops to cut off any retreat, an uncommon athlete will not turn back, and he keeps others from turning back as well.

An uncommon athlete also won't retreat at game time. Once he gets on the bus, once he arrives at the competition, there is no turning back until the mission is accomplished. She has a goal, and as long as there is time on the clock, she competes to win. The bigger the game, the brighter the lights, the stronger his or her willingness to fight to the end. That is uncommon nerve.

And an uncommon athlete doesn't retreat when obstacles come either. An injury, a new position, a new coach, a sudden change. Nothing that pops up in the uncommon athlete's life can send her backward. With each new challenge, he refuses to back down or give up. He keeps going until he achieves his goals. Uncommon athletes are the ones who call for "no retreat." They carry the flag. They raise the call. They lead their team forward, call them into the fight and refuse to turn back from any challenge.

Nerve is Strength

An athlete cannot display nerve without strength, but strength is not just how much you bench press or dead lift. While physical strength and stamina are important, strength is about much, much more than our body's ability to perform. True strength is an internal "courage, resolve or strength of character." It can also be called "grit."

"In the heart of a competitive battle it is your grit that has you push through that one play or one shot ... that can make all the difference in the outcome."[10] Grit is the tenacity to hold on and not let go. It's having the backbone to stand up to against a tough opponent, a tough play, a tough call. It's having the guts to play with everything you've got, no matter what. As Gandhi said, "Strength does not come from physical capacity. It comes from an indomitable will."[11] That is uncommon nerve.

Nerve is Vision

The uncommon athlete sees the world as full of opportunities, not roadblocks. Where others see hardship and an excuse to give up, an uncommon athlete seizes the chance to do something great in the face of great difficulty. It's the quarterback, down by 10 points in the fourth quarter, who rallies his team to come back. He is aware of the clock, the score and the other team, but instead of certain defeat, he sees the chance to do something amazing.

Bethany Hamilton had vision. In 2003, a tiger shark attacked while she was lying on her surfboard, and she lost her arm below the shoulder. In a single moment, her hopes of becoming a professional surfer seemed impossible, but three weeks after her accident, she was back in the water, learning how to surf with only one arm. In early 2004, she entered and won her first major surfing competition, and she continues to surf professionally. When most people would have let their dream die, Bethany Hamilton saw an opportunity to do something no one had ever done before. Instead of hanging up her board, she dove back in and saw her vision come true.[12]

No matter their circumstance, no matter where they came from, and no matter what they have experienced, uncommon athletes have a vision that drives them. They see every competition, every season and every challenge as a new possibility, and they reach forward to grab those chances. Like Bethany Hamilton, they decide from the very beginning they are going to make it, and they keep going, no matter what comes their way.

The Myths of Nerve

As powerful as uncommon nerve is though, and as much as we love to watch athletes compete with nerve, it is often misunderstood. Before we can truly gain nerve, we must also recognize what it is not.

Myth #1 - Nerve means working alone.
Some people imagine that uncommon nerve looks like a gunfighter in the Old West or a gladiator in the arena. It is one man (or woman) against the world, but nerve is not about going it alone. Yes, in the final moment, a great achievement will come down to you. You're the kicker facing the field goal your team needs to win. You stand at the starting line of the finals of the 100-yard dash. You're on the free throw line, lining up a shot in a loud arena. It's just you and the ball. You and the moment you have trained and practiced for. You have to do what you set out to do.

Nerve is simply the determination to do what you came to do in your moment of truth. And the uncommon athlete will rise to that challenge only when he has good support before and afterward that pivotal moment.[13]

Uncommon nerve happens *because* of those who stand with us, not in spite of them.[14] Parents and friends support us, sacrifice for us, cheer us on and encourage us when we're struggling. Coaches and trainers give advice and feedback, correct mistakes, teach us the skills and equip us with the tools we'll need when the crisis comes. We need this support. Without it, we will struggle instead of succeed, no matter how much nerve we have.

Myth #2 - Overconfidence is the same as Nerve.
Overconfidence is an exaggerated sense of your own abilities. It's a belief that nothing can drop you to the mat. It's cockiness; thinking you are more than enough to handle anything that comes your way. No one can touch you. But overconfidence is not nerve. As Bill Walsh said, "To a winner, complacency and overconfidence can be destructive."[15]

Uncommon nerve is built on a confidence that comes from an honest assessment of yourself. You know your strengths and weaknesses. You know that you, or your team, can do what you came to do, but you also know you cannot control everything. While overconfidence blows off all concerns, even legitimate ones, uncommon nerve knows the final score cannot be guaranteed.

> During the last two minutes of a close basketball game, during the last set of a close tennis match, or in a sudden death playoff in other sports, it really doesn't matter who is supposed to be better. It's who makes a play, gets a break, is in the best condition or wants to win the most. Talent does not guarantee victory.[16]

Nerve is never blustering. It is never overconfidence. It is simply the will to play hard and refuse to give up until the last buzzer sounds.

Myth #3 - Nerve is arrogance.
Arrogance is about demonstrating your own superiority. It's about toughing it out so you can point out how great you are. Arrogance is an attitude that looks down on others and is never the mark of an uncommon athlete.

Uncommon nerve is not arrogant. When you actually face a crisis moment, it rarely feels courageous. It doesn't feel commanding. Instead, you feel nervous, uncertain, even sick to your stomach. Arrogance claims it never feels those things. Nerve is the will to move *through* those feelings and rise to meet the challenge anyway. It's about finding strength when you thought you had nothing left. It's about giving your all to get to the other side and realizing that, despite all odds, you actually did it. And that experience doesn't make you arrogant. It makes you uncommon.

Just Keep Going

Like Dory in *Finding Nemo*, the secret to success is often "just keep swimming." When things are tough and obstacles come, you will feel like giving up. You will have many opportunities to walk away when things get hard, but uncommon nerve will hold you to your path. It will help you see your fight through to the end.

Whether it is a big game, a hard class, a tough decision or a family crisis, you can succeed. Michael Jordan was passed over for varsity in high school. Oprah Winfrey was once fired as a television reporter. Thomas Edison's teachers called him a failure in school, but because they had the nerve to keep pursuing their dreams, each one of them succeeded. They refused to let anything stop them. They fought back and fought through, and they became great. On the field and in life, you can live that uncommon nerve, too.

TALK About It

1. How are both adjustment and nerve necessary? Why can't you have only one or the other?

2. Why is determination so important in sports? What does it look like when an athlete lacks determination?

3. Do you struggle with fear? How do you deal with your fears when they rise? How does nerve help you overcome your fears?

4. Have you ever been tempted to give up or retreat? What kept you from doing it?

5. Which of the myths about uncommon nerve have you heard or believed? Why doesn't nerve make us arrogant or overconfident?

Conclusion: A Message to Parents

A New Era

We are living in a new era of sports, particularly for our youth. In recent years, our children's involvement in sports has become a year-round oppression that starts as early as preschool. In this new culture, parents are asked to commit their child to one sport and one sport only as soon as possible, and the pressure to become competitive comes earlier every year. Participation in any sport can be costly and time-consuming, and it often challenges and competes with important family values. On top of practices, games, and fundraisers, some parents are pressured to sacrifice their remaining family time on weekends for tournaments and other team activities.

For our children to become uncommon athletes though, they need more from their parents than simply going with the flow of this new sports culture. As parents, we too must choose an uncommon path so our sons and daughters can become the best athletes, students and people they can be.

Count The Cost

It's not enough to want our children to be uncommon athletes. Instead of being "sports parents" only, we must help them find the balance between fun and competition, between participation and a drive for success that undermines their integrity, their health, or their teammates. We need to parent our children, giving them clear direction and boundaries in sports and in life. We need to focus on more than just the cost of trainers, equipment and off-season travel teams.

I firmly believe sports participation is worth the cost. Competing in athletics offers our children valuable experiences and opportunities. It's important and fun and healthy, but we must choose to be parents, first. In raising an uncommon athlete, we have to be the ones who teach our child how to make tough choices, how to sacrifice now for a greater good later, and how to live selfless, understanding that the needs of the family come first.

Developing a Scholar Athlete

In addition, we have to teach our children to value education as much as sports. Unfortunately, in today's sports climate, parents are often so focused on talent, athletic ability and training that we downplay academics. We push for more playing time, a varsity slot, a college scholarship, but we need to have a realistic expectation of our children's abilities and accomplishments. We need to make sure they are realistic, too.

The truth is, the majority of high school athletes will not get a college scholarship and, of those who do, even fewer will play professional sports. According to the NCAA, a college football player has a 1.6% chance of making the NFL. A men's basketball player has a 1.1% chance of playing in the NBA, and a woman's basketball player has a 0.9% chance to make the WNBA.

As parents, we must teach our children to value and pursue their full education while they play sports. Whether they ever play at the highest level, nearly every athlete can graduate. In the NCAA study, "graduation success rates are 86% in Division I, 71% in Division II and 87% in Division III."[1] Most importantly, a complete education will benefit all of the child's life, for the rest of his life.

We have to help our children become scholar-athletes. Sports are important, but so is education. An uncommon athlete must learn to balance competition and the classroom, and parents must help their children develop that balance at every level.

Keep The Good in Sports

Lastly, parents must also be good role models for their athlete. Coaches and trainers play important roles in our children's lives, but parents are the primary influence on a child at every level of competition.

Parents of an uncommon athlete must be watchdogs. They are the gatekeepers. They ensure every athlete receives the positive life skills that are taught through sports participation, such as teamwork, self-discipline, commitment, leadership and being selfless.

Unfortunately, many parents do not have a positive influence. Instead of being positive, they are impulsive and unkind. They model attitudes and behaviors that are the opposite of what sports can teach our students. From the dads who fights with refs or other parents, to the moms who are willing to cheat so their athletes win, these parents actually prevent their children from gaining all that sports offer.

As parents, we too must choose the uncommon road. We have to model good judgment with the things we say in the stands and in our relationship with our child's coach. We have to remember that our children are watching us and will display the same behavior we exhibit at sporting events. We have to actually do the things we expect from our children. As parents we have to let the coaches coach, and we have to support all the players on the team.

As parents, we want our children to become uncommon athletes, and we play an active and important role in their development. By staying positive and modeling the qualities of PASSION we want our children to develop, we will help our child become the athlete, the scholar and the person he was meant to be.

NOTES

Introduction

1 Teddy Mitrosilis, "Emotional LeBron James Pays Tribute to Cleveland," FoxSports.com, June 19, 2016, http://www.foxsports.com/nba/story/cleveland-cavaliers-nba-title-lebron-james-honors-city-postgame-interview-061916.

2 Mark 8:36.

Chapter 1

1 Jerry Rice, "Jerry RiceEnshrinement Speech," Pro Football Hall of Fame, August 7, 2010, http://www.profootballhof.com/players/jerry-rice/enshrinement.

2 Proverbs 4:25.

3 Proverbs 15:20.

4 "Emmitt Smith," Pro Football Hall of Fame, http://www.profootballhof.com/players/emmitt-smith.

5 Emmitt Smith, "Emmitt Smith Enshrinement Speech," Pro Football Hall of Fame, August 7, 2010, http://www.profootballhof.com/players/emmitt-smith/enshrinement.

6 Aimee Berg, "With Bob Bowman's Help, Michael Phelps Achieves Everyday Excellence," LiveHappy.com, July 6, 2015, www.livehappy.com/self/fitness/bob-bowmans-help-michael-phelps-achieves-everyday-excellence.

7 Dewitt Robinson, "Dr. Benjamin E. Mays: Just A Minute," July 20, 2011, http://dewittrobinson.com/minute.

8 Psalm 90.

9 Fellowship of Christian Athletes, "FCA Magazine Exclusive with USA Track & Field's Allyson Felix," FCA video, June 24, 2016, http://fcaresources.com/video/allyson-felix.

10 Ross Atkins, "12 Quotes from Bobby Knight," ChristianScienceMonitor.com, October 25, 2012, http://www.csmonitor.com/The-Culture/2012/1025/12-quotes-from-coach-Bob-Knight/Preparation.

11 Zac Clark, "Jerry Rice's Legendary Hill Training," Stack.com, October 17, 2010, http://www.stack.com/a/jerry-rices-legendary-hill-training.

12 Alan Goldberg, "Big Game Preparation: 7 Tips to Staying Cool & Calm in the Clutch," Competitivedge.com, 2016, https://www.competitivedge.com/big-game-preparation-7-tips-staying-cool-calm-clutch.

13 Steve Nash, BrainyQuote.com, 2016, http://www.brainyquote.com/quotes/quotes/s/stevenash544773.html.

14 Gary Player, BrainyQuote.com, 2016, http://www.brainyquote.com/quotes/quotes/g/garyplayer101939.html.

Chapter 2

1 Jim Rome, "Lauren Hill Shares Her Story With Jim Rome," JimRome.com, October 17, 2014, http://jimrome.com/2014/10/17/lauren-hill-shares-her-story-with-jim-rome.

2 Ecclesiastes 11:2; Ecclesiastes 11:6.

3 Proverbs 14:15.

4 Brett Forrest, "How Ohio State's Braxton Miller Made the Move from Quarterback to Wide Reciever," ESPN.com, November 18, 2015, http://espn.go.com/college-football/story/_/id/14156636/how-ohio-state-braxton-miller-made-move-quarterback-wide-receiver.

5 Captain Ron, "2016 NFL Draft: Rick Smith, Bill O'Brien React to Drafting Braxton Miller & Nick Martin," BattleRedBlog.com, May 3, 2016, http://www.battleredblog.com/2016/5/3/11577242/2016-nfl-draft-rick-smith-bill-obrien-react-to-drafting-braxton.

6 Daniel 1:8.

7 "Risk, Protective and Resilience Factors for Children," ENCARE.info, 2007, http://www.encare.info/en-GB/riskyenvironments/resilience/factors.

8 Romans 5:3-4.

Chapter 3

1 "Carli Lloyd," *Wikipedia, The Free Encyclopedia*, May 21, 2016,

https://en.wikipedia.org/wiki/Carli_Lloyd.

2 Brian Saban, "STACK Athlete of the Year 2015: Carli Lloyd Surpassed All Expectations," Stack.com, December 21, 2015, www.stack.com/a/carli-lloyd-athlete-of-the-year.

3 Muhammad Ali, BrainyQuote.com, 2016, www.brainyquote.com/quotes/quotes/m/muhammadal148629.html.

4 Kareem Abdul-Jabbar, BrainyQuote.com, 2016, http://www.brainyquote.com/quotes/quotes/k/kareemabdu370653.html.

5 Ilyssa Panitz, "Gymnastic Gold: Interview with Shawn Johnson and Her Mom, Teri." Parents.com, 2012. http://www.parents.com/parenting/celebrity-parents/moms-dads/interview-with-shawn-johnson-olympics-gymnastics.

6 Ken Gordon, "After Losing His Wife, Stefanie, to Cancer, Chris Spielman Shares Their Story In New Book." ColumbusDispatch.com, April 17, 2012. http://www.dispatch.com/content/stories/life_and_entertainment/2012/04/17/the-latest-chapter.html.

7 Galatians 6:7-8.

8 Galatians 6:9.

9 Hebrews 12:11.

10 Robert Klemko, "So This is the NFL, Part II," The MMQB, July 9, 2014. http://mmqb.si.com/2014/07/09/nfl-rookie-symposium-part-2.

11 Hebrews 12:2.

12 Apolo Ohno, BrainyQuote.com, 2016, http://www.brainyquote.com/quotes/quotes/a/apoloohno543264.html, accessed August 21, 2016.

13 "Marion Jones," *Wikipedia, The Free Encyclopedia,* https://en.wikipedia.org/wiki/Marion_Jones.

14 "Vince Carter Got It Right," NYTimes.com, May 22, 2001, http://www.nytimes.com/2001/05/22/opinion/vince-carter-got-it-right.html?_r=0.

Chapter 4

1 "Mia Hamm," *Wikipedia, The Free Encyclopedia,* August 31, 2016, https://en.wikipedia.org/wiki/Mia_Hamm.

2 Mia Hamm, BrainyQuote.com, 2016,

http://www.brainyquote.com/quotes/quotes/m/miahamm20452
8.html.

3 Webster's Third New International Dictionary, Unabridged, s.v. "selfishness," accessed September 22, 2016, http://unabridged.merriam-webster.com.

4 Matthew 7:3-5.

5 Goldberg, "Serving Others."

6 Alan Goldberg, "Serving Others – The Lost Art of Champions," Competitive Advantage, 2016, https://www.competitivedge.com/"serving-others"---"-lost-art-champions."

7 Goldberg, "Serving Others."

8 Stanley Tucker, "Devotional of the Week: Selfish or Selfless," Sports Spectrum, January 14, 2015, http://www.sportsspectrum.com/articles/2015/01/14/devotional-of-the-week-selfish-or-selfless.

9 Isaiah Thomas, BrainyQuote.com, 2016, www.brainyquote.com/quotes/quotes/i/isaiahthom347043.html.

10 Goldberg, "Serving Others."

11 Goldberg, "Serving Others."

12 Michael Jordon, QuoteHD.com, 2016, http://www.quotehd.com/quotes/michael-jordan-quote-there-are-plenty-of-teams-in-every-sport-that-have-great.

13 Goldberg, "Serving Others."

14 Adrian Wojnarowski, "How Steph Curry Makes His Peace With a Contract Unfit for the MVP," Yahoo Sports, December 11, 2015, http://sports.yahoo.com/news/how-stephen-curry-makes-his-daily-peace-with-a-contract-unfit-for-the-mvp-014857274.html.

15 Wojnarowski, "How Steph Curry."

16 Philippians 2:3.

17 Philippians 2:4.

18 Aaron Torres, "Florida State Player's Incredible Gesture Will Bring You to Tears," NYPost.com, August 31, 2016, http://nypost.com/2016/08/31/florida-state-players-incredible-gesture-will-bring-you-to-tears.

19 Courtney Thompson, "Buckhorn HS Football Team Pitches in with Chores to Help Family Recover," WAFF.com, August 6, 2016, http://www.waff.com/story/32701336/buckhorn-hs-football-team-pitches-in-with-chores-to-help-family-recover.

20 Proverbs 18:12.

21 Brad Herzog, *Inspiring Stories of Sportsmanship* (Minneapolis, MN: Free Spirit Publishing, 2014), 85-88.

Chapter 5

1 David Brown, "Jeremy Affeldt Returns $500,000 to San Francisco Giants After Noticing Clerical Error In Contract," Yahoo Sports, May 15, 2013, http://sports.yahoo.com/blogs/mlb-big-league-stew/jeremy-affeldt-returns-500-000-san-francisco-giants-17403647 1.html.

2 Webster's Third New International Dictionary, Unabridged, s.v. "integrity," accessed October 24, 2016, http://unabridged.merriam-webster.com.

3 Proverbs 11:3.

4 Proverbs 13:6.

5 Proverbs 10:9.

6 Brad Herzog, *Inspiring Stories of Sportsmanship* (Minneapolis, MN: Free Spirit Publishers), 81-84.

7 Tim Brown, *Boys Won't Be Boys* (Xulon Press, 2013), 29.

8 Proverbs 22:1.

9 David Robinson, *Wikipedia, The Free Encyclopedia,* May 17, 2016, https://en.wikipedia.org/wiki/David_Robinson_%28basketball%2 9.

10 David Robinson, AZQuotes.com, Wind and Fly LTD, 2016. http://www.azquotes.com/quote/721533.

11 David Robinson, AZQuotes.com, Wind and Fly LTD, 2016. http://www.azquotes.com/quote/535079.

12 David Robinson, *Wikipedia.*

13 Alice Linahan, "A True Class Act ... "The Admiral" David Robinson Hall of Fame Speech," ActiveRain.com, September 16, 2009, http://activerain.com/blogsview/1240886/a-true-class-act----the-admiral-david-robinson-hall-of-fame-speech.

14 Chris Flynn, "Top 10 Most Disliked Athletes in America," TheRichest.com, August 3, 2015, http://www.therichest.com/sports/top-10-most-disliked-athletes-in-america.

15 Brown, *Boys Won't Be Boys*, 31.

16 *Remember the Titans*, Screenplay, https://docs.google.com/document/preview?hgd=1&id=1UsyTI

CR1VDY7b68V-kgoR99IVIXETnfFImFid2DTxI0, 45.

Chapter 6

1 Wilma Rudolph, *Wikipedia, The Free Encyclopedia*, May 24, 2016, https://en.wikipedia.org/wiki/Wilma_Rudolph.

2 Wilma Rudolph, BrainyQuote.com, 2016, http://www.brainyquote.com/quotes/quotes/w/wilmarudol1843 52.html.

3 Webster's Third New International Dictionary, Unabridged, s.v. "obstacle," accessed September 23, 2016, http://unabridged.merriam-webster.com.

4 "Tamika Catchings,"WNBA.com, 2016, http://www.wnba.com/player/tamika-catchings/#/panel-four.

5 David Kirkwood, "WNBA Star Tamika Catchings Has No Disability On the Hard Court," HearingHealthMatters.com, September 28, 2011, http://hearinghealthmatters.org/hearingnewswatch/2011/wnba-star-tamika-catchings-has-no-disability-on-the-hard-court.

6 Marguerite Ward, "Olympic Gold Medalist and WNBA MVP: How Burnout Actually Helped My Career," CNBC.com, August 25, 2016, http://www.cnbc.com/2016/08/25/olympic-gold-medalist-elena-delle-donne-burnout-helped-my-career.html.

7 William Arthur Ward, BrainyQuote.com, 2016, http://www.brainyquote.com/quotes/quotes/w/williamart100517 .html.

8 Bob Feller, BrainyQuote.com, 2016, http://www.brainyquote.com/quotes/quotes/b/bobfeller139608. html.

9 Lysa Terkeurst, "The Sting of Rejection," Focus on the Family Magazine, Aug/Sept. 2016, 37.

10 Pat Riley, BrainyQuote.com, 2016, http://www.brainyquote.com/quotes/quotes/p/patriley147924.ht ml.

11 Lysa Terkeurst, "The Sting of Rejection," 37.

12 Apis Communication Science, "Blame, Empathy, and Brené Brown's Infamous Brew-tastrophe," ApisCommunicationScience.com, January 4, 2016, https://apiscommunicationscience.wordpress.com/tag/brene-brown-on-blame.

13 James 1:3-4.

14 Hebrews 11:1.

15 Warren Weirsbe, *Be Amazed* (Colorado Springs, CO: David C Cook, 2004), 136.

16 W. Clement Stone, BrainyQuote.com, 2016, http://www.brainyquote.com/quotes/quotes/w/wclements15572 8.html.

17 History Channel Staff, "Gertrude Ederle Becomes First Woman to Swim English Channel," History.com, 2009, http://www.history.com/this-day-in-history/gertrude-ederle-becomes-first-woman-to-swim-english-channel.

18 Team Hoyt Home Page, http://teamhoyt.com.

19 Kirkwood, "WNBA Star Tamika Catchings."

20 Ward, "Olympic Gold Medalist and WNBA MVP."

21 Michael Jordan, BrainyQuote.com, 2016, http://www.brainyquote.com/quotes/quotes/m/michaeljor16596 7.html.

Chapter 7

1 "Jeffrey Julmis Tumbles During Hurdles, Gets Up and Finishes," NBColympics.com, August 17, 2016, http://www.nbcolympics.com/video/jeffrey-julmis-tumbles-during-hurdles-gets-and-finishes.

2 Nelson Mandela, BrainyQuote.com, 2016, http://www.brainyquote.com/quotes/quotes/n/nelsonmand1787 89.html.

3 Jack Nicklaus, BrainyQuote.com, 2016, http://www.brainyquote.com/quotes/quotes/j/jacknickla379304. html.

4 Philippians 4:6.

5 Jack Nicklaus, BrainyQuote.com, 2016, http://www.brainyquote.com/quotes/quotes/j/jacknickla400460. html.

6 Howard Falco, "Grit, Grind and Mind: The Path of a Champion," The Huffington Post, June 23, 2015, http://www.huffingtonpost.com/howard-falco/grit-grind-and-mind-the-p_1_b_7648672.html.

7 Jason Fell, "15 Motivational Quotes from Legends in Sports,"

Entrepreneur.com, April 1, 2015,
https://www.entrepreneur.com/slideshow/244486.

8 Paul Bryant, BrainyQuote.com, 2016,
http://www.brainyquote.com/quotes/quotes/p/paulbryant19278
2.html.

9 Bill Rabinowitz, "NBA: Injuries Haven't Hurt Redd's
Determination," The Columbus Dispatch, October 22, 2010,
http://www.dispatch.com/content/stories/sports/2010/10/22/in
juries-havent-hurt-redds-determination.html.

10 Falco, "Grit, Grind and Mind."

11 Mahatma Gandhi, BrainyQuote.com, 2016,
http://www.brainyquote.com/quotes/quotes/m/mahatmagan122
084.html.

12 Mark Clark, "Soul Surfer Interview With Bethany Hamilton."
WhatCulture.com, September 24, 2011,
http://whatculture.com/film/soul-surfer-interview-with-bethany-
hamilton.

13 Proverbs 28:26.

14 Proverbs 15:22.

15 Bill Walsh, AZQuotes.com, 2016,
http://www.azquotes.com/quote/670251.

16 Jim Brown, "When Overconfidence meets Reality,"
Southern.USTA.com, September 20, 2004,
http://www.southern.usta.com/News/Sport-Science-
News/2004_09/106460_When_Overconfidence_Meets_Reality.

Conclusion
1NCAA, "Estimated Probability of Competing in Professional
Athletics," NCAA.org, April 25, 2016,
http://www.ncaa.org/about/resources/research/estimated-
probability-competing-professional-athletics

Bibliography

Apis Communication Science. "Blame, Empathy, and Brené Brown's
Infamous Brew-tastrophe."
January 4, 2016.
https://apiscommunicationscience.wordpress.com/tag/brene-
brown-on-blame/, accessed August 26, 2016.

Apolo Ohno. BrainyQuote.com, Xplore Inc, 2016.
http://www.brainyquote.com/quotes/quotes/a/
apoloohno543264.html, accessed August 21, 2016.

Associated Press. "Weeks after wife's death, ex-Detroit Lions
linebacker Chris Spielman enters College
Football Hall of Fame." Mlive.com. December 9, 2009.
http://www.mlive.com/lions/index.ssf/2009/12/former_detroit_li
ons_linebacke.html, accessed May 16, 2016.

Atkin, Ross. "12 Quotes from Bobby Knight." October 25, 2012.
ChristianScienceMonitor.com.
http://www.csmonitor.com/The-Culture/2012/1025/12-quotes-
from-coach-Bob-Knight/Preparation, accessed August 29, 2016.

Berg, Aimee. "With Bob Bowman's Help, Michael Phelps Achieves
Everyday Excellence." Live
Happy.com. July 6, 2015. www.livehappy.com/self/fitness/bob-
bowmans-help-michael-phelps-achieves-everyday-excellence,
accessed May 18, 2016.

"Bethany Hamilton." *Wikipedia, The Free Encyclopedia.* June 1, 2016.
https://en.wikipedia.org/wiki/Bethany_Hamilton, accessed May 14,
2016.

Bill Walsh. AZQuotes.com, Wind and Fly LTD, 2016.
http://www.azquotes.com/quote/670251,
accessed September 09, 2016.

Bob Feller. BrainyQuote.com, Xplore Inc, 2016.
http://www.brainyquote.com/quotes/quotes/b/
bobfeller139608.html, accessed September 25, 2016.

Booker T. Washington. BrainyQuote.com, Xplore Inc, 2016.
http://www.brainyquote.com/quotes/
quotes/b/bookertwa139251.html, accessed August 26, 2016.

"Braxton Miller." *Wikipedia, The Free Encyclopedia.*
https://en.wikipedia.org/wiki/Braxton_Miller,
accessed May 13, 2016.

Brown, Brené. *Daring Greatly.* New York: Avery, 2012.

Brown, David. "Jeremy Affeldt Returns $500,000 to San Francisco
Giants After Noticing Clerical
Error In Contract." Yahoo Sports. May 15, 2013.
http://sports.yahoo.com/blogs/mlb-big-league-stew/jeremy-
affeldt-returns-500-000-san-francisco-giants-174036471.html,
accessed May 15, 2016.

Brown, Jim. "When Overconfidence meets Reality." Southern.USTA.com. September 20, 2004. http://www.southern.usta.com/News/Sport-Science News/2004_09/ 106460_When_ Overconfidence_ Meets_Reality, accessed September 9, 2016.

Brown, Tim. *Boys Won't Be Boys.* Xulan Press, 2013.

Capt Ron. "2016 NFL Draft: Rick Smith, Bill O'Brien React To Drafting Braxton Miller & Nick Martin." Battle Red Blog. May 3, 2016. http://www.battleredblog.com/2016/5/3/11577242/ 2016-nfl-draft-rick-smith-bill-obrien-react-to-drafting-braxton, accessed May 20, 2016.

"Carli Lloyd." *Wikipedia, The Free Encyclopedia.* May 21, 2016. https://en.wikipedia.org/wiki/Carli_Lloyd, accessed June 3, 2016.

"Chris Spielman." *Wikipedia, The Free Encyclopedia.* May 12, 2016. Accessed May 16, 2016. https://en.wikipedia.org/wiki/Chris_Spielman, accessed May 16, 2016.

Clark, Mark. "Soul Surfer Interview With Bethany Hamilton." WhatCulture.com. September 24, 2011. http://whatculture.com/film/soul-surfer-interview-with-bethany-hamilton, accessed May 14, 2016.

Clark, Zac. "Jerry Rice's Legendary Hill Training." STACK.com. October 17, 2010. http://www.stack.com/a/jerry-rices-legendary-hill-training, accessed May 14, 2016.

Clear, James. "40 Years of Stanford Research Found That People With This One Quality Are More Likely to Succeed." 2016. http://jamesclear.com/delayed-gratification, accessed August 23, 2016.

David Robinson. AZQuotes.com, Wind and Fly LTD, 2016. http://www.azquotes.com/quote/721533, accessed May 22, 2016.

David Robinson. AZQuotes.com, Wind and Fly LTD, 2016. http://www.azquotes.com/quote/535079, accessed May 22, 2016.

David Robinson. *Wikipedia, The Free Encyclopedia.* May 17, 2016. https://en.wikipedia.org/wiki/David_Robinson_%28basketball%29, accessed May 20, 2016.

"Emmitt Smith." Pro Football Hall of Fame.
http://www.profootballhof.com/players/emmitt-smith/,
accessed May 18, 2016.

Falco, Howard. "Grit, Grind and Mind: The Path of a Champion."
The Huffington Post.com. June 23,
2015. http://www.huffingtonpost.com/howard-falco/grit-grind-and-
mind-the-p_1_b_7648672.html, accessed September 1, 2016.

Fell, Jason. "15 Motivational Quotes from Legends in Sports."
Entrepreneur.com. April 1, 2015.
https://www.entrepreneur.com/slideshow/244486, accessed
September 22, 2016.

Fellowship of Christian Athletes. "FCA Magazine Exclusive with USA
Track & Field 's Allyson
Felix." FCA video 2:22. June 24, 2016.
http://fcaresources.com/video/allyson-felix.

Flynn, Chris. "Top 10 Most Disliked Athletes in America."
Therichest.com. August 3, 2015.
http://www.therichest.com/sports/top-10-most-disliked-athletes-in-
america/, accessed August 25, 2016.

Forrest, Brett. "How Ohio State's Braxton Miller Made the Move
from Quarterback to Wide Receiver."
ESPN.com. November 18, 2015. http://espn.go.com/college-
football/story/_/id/14156636/how-ohio-state-braxton-miller-mad
e-move-quarterback-wide-receiver, accessed May 13, 2016.

Ganguli, Tania. "Cloaked in secrecy, Braxton Miller switched to WR
to prepare for his NFL dream."
ESPN.com. May 7, 2016.
http://espn.go.com/nfl/story/_/id/15468307/nfl-braxton-miller-
covert-plan-helped-realize-nfl-dream-houston-texans, accessed June
3, 2016.

Gordon, Ken. "After Losing His Wife, Stefanie, to Cancer, Chris
Spielman Shares Their Story In New
Book." The Columbus Dispatch. April 17, 2012.
http://www.dispatch.com/content/stories/
life_and_entertainment/2012/04/17/the-latest-chapter.html,
accessed May 12, 2016.

Gary Player. BrainyQuote.com, Xplore Inc, 2016.
http://www.brainyquote.com/quotes/quotes/g/
garyplayer101939.html, accessed September 21, 2016.

Goldberg, Alan. "Big Game Preparation: 7 Tips to Staying Cool & Calm in the Clutch." Competitveedge.com. 2016. https://www.competitivedge.com/big-game-preparation-7-tips-staying-cool-calm-clutch, accessed August 20, 2016.

—. "Serving Others – The Lost Art of Champions." Competitive Advantage. 2016. https://www.competitivedge.com/"serving-others"—"-lost-art-champions," accessed August 24, 2016.

Goyanes, Cristina. "U.S. Women's Soccer Star Carli Lloyd's 17-Year Plan to Become the World's Greatest Athlete." Shape.com. November 2, 2015. http://www.shape.com/celebrities/interviews/us-womens-soccer-star-carli-lloyds-17-year-plan-become-worlds-greatest, accessed August 20, 2016.

Ha, Samuel. "Top 30 Greatest Fear Quotes." MightyFighter.com. 2016. http://www.mightyfighter.com/top-30-greatest-fear-quotes, accessed August 27, 2016.

Herzog, Brad. "Ace of Hearts." In *Inspiring Stories of Sportsmanship*, 85-88. Minneapolis, MN: Free Spirit Publishing, 2014.

—. "Record Re-Set." In *Inspiring Stories of Sportsmanship*, 81-84. Minneapolis, MN: Free Spirit Publishers, 2014.

History Channel Staff. "Gertrude Ederle Becomes First Woman To Swim English Channel." History.com. 2009. http://www.history.com/this-day-in-history/gertrude-ederle-becomes-first-woman-to-swim-english-channel, accessed June 1, 2016.

Isaiah Thomas. BrainyQuote.com, Xplore Inc, 2016. http://www.brainyquote.com/quotes/quotes/i/isaiahthom347043.html, accessed August 26, 2016.

Jack Nicklaus. BrainyQuote.com, Xplore Inc, 2016. http://www.brainyquote.com/quotes/quotes/j/jacknickla379304.html, accessed September 25, 2016.

—. BrainyQuote.com, Xplore Inc, 2016. http://www.brainyquote.com/quotes/quotes/j/jacknickla400460.html, accessed September 25, 2016.

"Jeffrey Julmis Tumbles During Hurdles, Gets Up and Finishes."

NBColympics.com. August 17, 2016.
http://www.nbcolympics.com/video/jeffrey-julmis-tumbles-during-hurdles-gets-and-finishes, accessed September 22, 2016.
"Jerry Rice," *Wikipedia, The Free Encyclopedia,*
https://en.wikipedia.org/wiki/Jerry_Rice, accessed
May 14, 2016.
Kareem Abdul-Jabbar. BrainyQuote.com, Xplore Inc, 2016.
http://www.brainyquote.com/quotes/
quotes/k/kareemabdu370653.html, accessed August 21, 2016.
Kirkwood, David. "WNBA Star Tamika Catchings Has No Disability
On the Hard Court."
HHTM.com. September 28, 2011.
http://hearinghealthmatters.org/hearingnewswatch/2011/ wnba-star-tamika-catchings-has-no-disability-on-the-hard-court, accessed
May 14, 2016.
Klemko, Robert. So This is the NFL, Part 1. The MMQB. July 8,
2014.
http://mmqb.si.com/2014/07/08/nfl-rookie-symposium-part-1,
accessed May 15, 2016.
–. So This is the NFL, Part II. The MMQB. July 9, 2014.
http://mmqb.si.com/2014/07/09/nfl-rookie-symposium-part-2,
accessed May 15, 2016.
Linahan, Alice. "A True Class Act ... "The Admiral" David Robinson
Hall of Fame Speech."
Activerain.com. September 16, 2009.
http://activerain.com/blogsview/1240886/a-true-class-act----
the-admiral–david-robinson-hall-of-fame-speech, accessed May 15,
2016.
Mahatma Gandhi. BrainyQuote.com, Xplore Inc, 2016.
http://www.brainyquote.com/quotes/quotes/m/
mahatmagan122084.html, accessed September 25, 2016.
"Marion Jones." *Wikipedia, The Free Encyclopedia,*
https://en.wikipedia.org/wiki/Marion_Jones,
accessed August 20, 2016.
Mia Hamm. BrainyQuote.com, Xplore Inc, 2016.
http://www.brainyquote.com/quotes/quotes/m/
miahamm204528.html, accessed August 22, 2016.
"Mia Hamm." *Wikipedia, the Free Encyclopedia.* August 31, 2016.
https://en.wikipedia.org/wiki/Mia_Hamm, accessed September 5,

2016.

Michael Jordan. BrainyQuote.com, Xplore Inc, 2016.
    http://www.brainyquote.com/quotes/quotes/m/
    michaeljor165967.html, accessed August 26, 2016.

Michael Jordon. QuoteHD.com. 2016.
    http://www.quotehd.com/quotes/michael-jordan-quote-there-
    are-plenty-of-teams-in-every-sport-that-have-great, accessed August
    22, 2016.

Muhammad Ali. BrainyQuote.com, Xplore Inc, 2016.
    http://www.brainyquote.com/quotes/quotes/m/
    muhammadal148629.html, accessed September 22, 2016.

NCAA. "Estimated Probability of Competing in Professional
    Athletics." NCAA.org. April 25, 2016.
    http://www.ncaa.org/about/resources/research/estimated-
    probability-competing-professional-athletics, accessed October 14,
    2016.

Nelson Mandela. BrainyQuote.com, Xplore Inc, 2016.
    http://www.brainyquote.com/quotes/quotes/n/
    nelsonmand178789.html, accessed September 25, 2016.

NHS Choices. "Ten Ways to Fight Your Fears." 2016.
    http://www.nhs.uk/Conditions/stress-anxiety-
    depression/Pages/overcoming-fears.aspx, accessed August 27, 2016.

Panitz, Ilyssa. "Gymnastic Gold: Interview with Shawn Johnson and
    Her Mom, Teri." Parents.com,
    2012. http://www.parents.com/parenting/celebrity-parents/moms-
    dads/interview-with-shawn-johnson-olympics-gymnastics, accessed
    August 22, 2016.

Pat Riley. BrainyQuote.com, Xplore Inc, 2016.
    http://www.brainyquote.com/quotes/quotes/p/patriley147924.html,
    accessed August 26, 2016.

Paul Bryant. BrainyQuote.com, Xplore Inc, 2016.
    http://www.brainyquote.com/quotes/quotes/p/
    paulbryant192782.html, accessed September 25, 2016.

Rabinowitz, Bill. "NBA: Injuries Haven't Hurt Redd's Determination."
    The Columbus Dispatch.
    October 22, 2010.
    http://www.dispatch.com/content/stories/sports/2010/10/22/inj
    uries-havent-hurt-redds-determination.html, accessed May 14, 2016.

Remember the Titans. Screenplay, 45.

https://docs.google.com/document/preview?
hgd=1&id=1UsyTICRlVDY7b68V-kgoR99IVIXETnfFImFid2DTxI0,
accessed May 15, 2016.

Rice, Jerry. "Jerry Rice Enshrinement Speech." Pro Football Hall of
Fame. August 7, 2010.
http://www.profootballhof.com/players/jerry-rice/enshrinement/,
accessed May 14, 2016.

Ridenaur, Marla. "Chris Spielman Bears All In Book About Wife's
Cancer Battle." Ohio.com. April
22, 2012. http://www.ohio.com/news/top-stories/marla-ridenour-
chris-spielman-bears-all-in-book-about-wife-s-cancer-battle-1.30223
8, accessed May 16, 2016.

"Risk, Protective and Resilience Factors for Children." ENCARE.info.
2007.
http://www.encare.info/en-
GB/riskyenvironments/resilience/factors/

Robinson, Dewitt. "Dr. Benjamin E. Mays: Just A Minute." July 20,
2011.
http://dewittrobinson.com/minute/

Rome, Jim. "Lauren Hill Shares Her Story With Jim Rome." The Jim
Rome Show. October 17, 2014.
http://jimrome.com/2014/10/17/lauren-hill-shares-her-story-with-
jim-rome, accessed May 13, 2016.

Sabin, Brian. "STACK Athlete of the Year 2015: Carli Lloyd Surpassed
All Expectations." Stack.com.
December 21, 2015. http://www.stack.com/a/carli-lloyd-athlete-of-
the-year, accessed May 16, 2016.

"Sixth Man." *Wikipedia, The Free Encyclopedia.* April 20, 2016.
https://en.wikipedia.org/wiki/Sixth_man, accessed May 13, 2016.

Smith, Emmitt. "Emmitt Smith Enshrinement Speech." August 7,
2010. Pro Football Hall of Fame.
http://www.profootballhof.com/players/emmitt-
smith/enshrinement, accessed May 18, 2016.

Steve Nash. BrainyQuote.com, Xplore Inc, 2016.
http://www.brainyquote.com/quotes/quotes/s/
stevenash544773.html, accessed September 21, 2016.

Tamika Catchings. WNBA. 2016.
http://www.wnba.com/player/tamika-catchings/#/panel-four,
accessed May 14, 2016.

"Team Hoyt." *Wikipedia, The Free Encyclopedia.* March 6, 2016. https://en.wikipedia.org/wiki/Team_Hoyt, accessed May 25, 2016.

Team Hoyt Home Page. Accessed May 25, 2016. http://teamhoyt.com.

Terkeurst, Lysa. "The Sting of Rejection." pp. 36-38. *Focus on the Family Magazine.* Aug/Sept. 2016.

Thompson, Courtney. "Buckhorn HS Football Team Pitches In With Chores to Help Family Recover." WAFF.com. August 6, 2016. http://www.waff.com/story/32701336/buckhorn-hs-football-team-pitches-in-with-chores-to-help-family-recover, accessed September, 22, 2016.

Torres, Aaron. "Florida State Player's Incredible Gestures Will Bring You To Tears." NYPost.com. August 31, 2016. http://nypost.com/2016/08/31/florida-state-players-incredible-gesture-will-bring-you-to-tears, accessed September 22, 2016.

Tucker, Stanley. "Devotional of the Week: Selfish or Selfless." Sports Spectrum. January 14, 2015. http://www.sportsspectrum.com/articles/2015/01/14/devotional-of-the-week-selfish-or-selfless/, accessed August 24. 2016.

Van Riper, Tom. "America's Most Disliked Athletes." Forbes.com. February 7, 2012. http://www.forbes.com/sites/tomvanriper/2012/02/07/americas-most-disliked-athletes/#5f4cd41cb215, accessed August 25, 2016.

"Vince Carter Got It Right." NYTimes.com. May 22, 2001. http://www.nytimes.com/2001/05/22/opinion/vince-carter-got-it-right.html?_r=0, accessed August 30, 2016.

W. Clement Stone. BrainyQuote.com, Xplore Inc, 2016. http://www.brainyquote.com/quotes/quotes/w/wclements155728.html, accessed August 26, 2016.

Ward, Marguerite. "Olympic Gold Medalist and WNBA MVP: How Burnout Actually Helped My Career." CNBC.com. August 25, 2016. http://www.cnbc.com/2016/08/25/olympic-gold-medalist-elena-delle-donne-burnout-helped-my-career.html, accessed August 26, 2016.

Warren Wiersbe. *Be Amazed.* David C Cook, Colorado Springs, CO. 2004. pg. 136

Wartenberg, Steve. "Stefanie Speilman's Legacy." *Columbus Monthly.* August 2011. http://www.columbusmonthly.com/content/stories/2011/08/stefani e-spielman039s-legacy.html, accessed May 16, 2016.

Weber, Andrew. "Braxton Miller Still Adjusting To Life As Ohio State Receiver." FoxSports.com. August 22, 2015. FoxSports.com. http://www.foxsports.com/college-football/story/ohio-state-buckeyes-braxton-miller-wide-receiver-update-082215, accessed May 13, 2016.

William Arthur Ward. BrainyQuote.com, Xplore Inc, 2016. http://www.brainyquote.com/quotes/quotes/w/williamart100517.html, accessed August 26, 2016.

Wilma Rudolph. BrainyQuote.com, Xplore Inc, 2016. http://www.brainyquote.com/quotes/quotes/w/wilmarudol184352.html, accessed September 23, 2016.

"Wilma Rudolph." *Wikipedia, The Free Encyclopedia.* May 24, 2016. https://en.wikipedia.org/wiki/Wilma_Rudolph, accessed May 29, 2016.

Wojnarowski, Adrian. "How Steph Curry Makes His Peace With a Contract Unfit for the MVP." Yahoo Sports. December 11, 2015. http://sports.yahoo.com/news/how-stephen-curry-makes-his-daily-peace-with-a-contract-unfit-for-the-mvp-014857274.html, accessed May 13, 2016.